# The Great Commission in Context

## Being Together with God's Creation

*Edited by*
**Santhosh S Kumar**

The United Theological College

&

Christian World Imprints™

First Published in 2016 by

**The United Theological College**
63 Millers Road, Benson Town
**Bangalore-560046**
utcprincipal@rediffmail.com
www.utc.edu.in
Phone: +91 80 23330015

&

**Christian World Imprints**(TM)
*Christian Publishing & Books from India*
H-12 Bali Nagar, **New Delhi-110015**
info@christianworldimprints.com
www.ChristianWorldImprints.com
Phone: +91 11 25465925

ISBN: 978-93-5148-148-5 (HB)
ISBN: 978-93-5148-149-2 (PB)



Printed in India.

# FOREWORD

The United Theological College, Bangalore, is pleased to continue its publication. It is no secret that UTC has housed many theologies, produced scholars and scholarly and text books. A rich heritage often is spoken and written about. Yes indeed it is true and following this legacy many books have been published by my colleagues. Among the many programmes UTC runs, the one which is much sought after is the refreshers programme which meets every year. It is a joy to see many of our alumni attending the programme - a time of not only renewing our fellowship, catching up with both professional and person news, but a time of rich learning from their experiences. Their presence provokes us to evaluate our curriculum and pedagogy of teaching. On the lighter side, it is like our children coming home... Indeed it is a joy to have them back....

This year the Convener and the Faculty of UTC took a decision to bring out a publication of all the papers presented on the theme 'Being Together: Fulfilling the Great Commission in Context'. Most of the presenters were UTC alumni involved in teaching, pastoring churches or holding positions in different institutions. The papers stem from the reflection of their own experiences and faith. The focus again is on the contemporary situation and context, challenging the readers to revisit the approaches, communication skills, priorities in sharing and understanding of the Gospel. Their emphasis is to remove the gospel from the closet of proclamation only and to expose the wholistic nature of gospel whose goal is transformation of the whole being in relation to nature and to strengthen the relationship with one to another, in order to bring about the wellbeing of humans as well as the bio sphere. This book challenges us to understand the great commission, live and share the gospel in action. Taking risks to present the gospel in today's language, style and worship meaningfully which calls for a rethinking of our present liturgy, creeds and traditions. Gospel in action means to be involved in the struggles of people than being passive, complacent, yielding to conspiracy of silence, conforming to the existing values and competition, preserving one's status and standards which is contrary to the values of the gospel.

I commend the efforts of the Convener and Editor Dr. Santhosh S Kumar to bring this publication in partnership with Christian World Imprints. I recommend this book to the readers to gain wholistic understanding of the Great Commission and sharing the contents of our rich faith in order to pave a way for a peaceful co-existence of human life with planet earth where there is no exploitation, manipulation and destruction of human life and nature.

**Dr. Nalini Arles**
Convener of the Publication Committee
11.03.2016

# PREFACE

Although Christianity had its humble origins in Asia, the cradle of multiple ancient religious faiths and cultures, it eventually got set into a rigid, western, affluent framework whereby all ensuing missionary enterprises were geared up for an aggressive evangelization campaign in a so-called 'western outfit'. Evangelization in due course became a synonym for westernization and coercive conversion. It was so misconstrued to communicate drastic deviation of people from their own philosophy of life, faith-orientation and indigenous culture they were embedded in. Most missionaries in being devout in their passion for proclaiming the good news turned myopic to the contextual settings they were in. Their orientations and compulsions were such that they were rigid in their approach to 'the other' right in front of them. Apart from exceptional cases the general missionary mindset was not attuned to discovering the mysteries in other religious cultures and traditions. While remaining keen and assiduous in unraveling the ***Sitz im Leben*** of the Scriptures, they watered down the equally significant efforts they ought to have rendered towards contextualizing the good news for different listeners in diverse contexts. The United Theological College since its inception in 1910 has been viewed as a college with a difference in terms of its goals and objectives. It is committed to academic excellence without compromising on its determination to identify with rural and marginalized communities in the society. Its annual academic guidance programme continues to embrace students of marginalized communities deprived of urban education, and extends to them the right orientation for a meaningful theological education. Having been granted the autonomous status by the Senate of Serampore College since 1976 it has been making all possible efforts to enrich its curriculum by striking the right balance between academic and experiential components in ministerial training. Issues on environment have been given due prominence in the curriculum. UTC works hand in hand with Churches and NGOs for the societal involvement of the students, which is a requirement to complete the study. The Annual Refreshment Course brings in first hand information about challenges confronted by the Indian society both urban and rural. The ecumenical students at UTC also bring in their input on issues confronted by their respective societies. As this book is published my sincere thanks to the scholars who contributed their writings and hope that this enterprise would assist the church reviewing its mission approaches and fulfill the Great Commission in more committed, generous, and effective manner.

**Rev. Dr. J. R. John Samuel Raj**
Principal
The United Theological College, Bangalore
25.05.2016

# A NOTE FROM THE EDITOR

Since a good introduction on the theme and the background of this publication is already given, I use this space primarily to thank the contributors of this book. This collection of essays by eminent personalities is an outcome of the UTC Alumni Refresher Programme 2015; and it discusses the various dimensions of the refresher theme 'Being Together: Fulfilling the Great Commission in Context'.

In this book, Dr. P. T. George sets the groundwork for the discussion by giving an apt introduction to the theme and HG Metropolitan Yuhanon Mor Meletius explains the Biblical foundation and understanding of the Great Commission. Thereafter, Dr. Paulraj Dayanandan gives a thorough exposition on the Good News in relation to science and the whole creation and Dr. Gnana Patrick challenges the readers to join in the public sphere in this mission with the Spirit of God. Dr. Jacob Kurien brings before us the considerations that are needed while trying to commit ourselves to the Great Commission in a world of many faiths and Dr. Sham P. Thomas leads the topic in discussion to a context of emerging media. Subsequently, Mr. Siddhartha explains the present deplorable state of the bionetwork and our necessary involvement in bringing God's creation to flourishing and Dr. Arul Dhas discusses the importance of health and wholeness of a person as intended by God with regard to the Great Commission. Dr. Mervin Shinoj Boas explicate the theological framework on the concept of being together and Dr. K. Jesurathnam visits the justice issues in the church and society. In conclusion, Dr. Kaholi Zhimomi re-visits the ecumenical priorities of the Indian churches in the context of the Great Commission and Rev. Viji Varghese Eapen reimages Christian worship in the light of the Great Commission proposing reformed approaches from alter and pulpit. My sincere thanks to these scholars who spent much time in reflecting on these sub-themes and contributing these scholarly writings.

I also thank Rev Anilal M. Jose, Mr. Aby K. Thomas, and Mr. Basil Baby Paul who took much effort to document the speeches of Dr. Sham P. Thomas, Mr. Siddhartha, and Dr. Paulraj Dayanandan respectively which are published after getting consent from the presenters. I am grateful to Dr. John Samuel Raj, the Principal of the United Theological College for writing the Preface and Dr. Nalini Arles, the Convener of the Publication Committee for writing a fitting Foreword. A special thanks to

Mr. Sudhanshu Kanda for facilitating this publication in collaboration with the Christian World Imprints.

With these dedications, I present this book to the readers with the hope that it would assist the churches in India in reviewing their approaches and strategies in their attempts to fulfill the Command of Jesus Christ in a more committed, generous and effective manner.

**Santhosh S Kumar**

# CONTENTS

*Chapter 1*

# BEING TOGETHER
## FULFILLING THE GREAT COMMISSION IN CONTEXT

**P. T. George**[1]

"Missions is the overflow of our delight in God because missions is the overflow of God's delight in being God." "To belong to Jesus is to embrace the nations with Him."

– John Piper

### 1. Introduction

Today we are living in a context that the religious fundamentalism reaches its peak and most of the faiths (religions) in the world become missionary that seriously engaged in adding more numbers to their flock. Gharvapasi and the growing persecution of Christians and missionaries are a few challenges that we face today. Migration and refugees are the realities even in our local context. Recently the WCC reminds us about another facet of today's context and the relevance of Christian Mission saying,

> "We are living in a world in which faith in mammon threatens the credibility of the gospel. Market ideology is spreading the propaganda

1 Rev. Dr. P. T. George is a leading Indian missiologist. Presently he is the Principal of the Kerala United Theological Seminary, Trivandrum.

that the global market will save the world through unlimited growth. This myth is a threat not only to economic life but also to the spiritual life of people, and not only to humanity but also to the whole creation. How can we proclaim the good news and values of God's kingdom in the global market or win over the spirit of the market? What kind of missional action can the church take in the midst of economic and ecological injustice and crisis on a global scale?"[2]

The modern mission theologians and the missionary engagements use of the concept of mission and missionary engagements were linked to the world order that was Eurocentric and hegemonic in nature and practice. Today, it seems that in the changing globalised and glocalised world order such expressions and praxis are outdated and a new paradigm and perspective in mission has to be emerged in the concept of missional thinking and engagements especially in the changing socio-political, religious and economic scenario of India. In this juncture, a fresh look at the great commission given by Jesus in relation with two new mission paradigms ***"Extensio Dei"*** (divine self reaching out), and *philoxenia* or *philexinos* (hospitality) will be pertinent in engaging with the existential challenges that threaten our missionary vocation as well as daily lives in context today.

## 2. Etymological Overview of the Term: Great Commission

It is unknown who coined the term "The Great Commission". It was likely first used as a summary for the passage by Dutch missionary, Justinian von Welz (1621-1688) but it was popularized by Hudson Taylor[3]. Hence, this usage is hardly 400 years old. It never called great commission in the Bible anywhere. The Great Commission is the instruction of the resurrected Jesus Christ to his disciples that they should continue to make disciples of all the nations as he started already. The most famous version of the Great Commission is in Matthew 28:18-20 and the other three gospels and Acts of the Apostles also narrated the same with different emphases. Mark 16:15 (... preach the good news to all creation); Luke 24:46-48 (... repentance and forgiveness of sins will be preached in His name to all nations... you are witnesses of these things); John 20:21 "... as the Father has send me, I am sending you"; Acts 1:8 (... and you will be my witnesses ...").

In Old Testament also one could see many parallel to the New Testament Great Commission such as Gen. 12: 1-3; Exo.19:4-6, Iss. 42:6, 49:6, 8 and so on. But, in this brief study I will be focusing more on the great commission passage given in Matthew.

2 "Together Towards Life: Mission and Evangelism in Changing Landscapes" www.oikoumene.org/.../together-towards-life-mission-and-evangelism, p. 7 (retrieved on 25.10.2015).

3 Castleman, Robbie F. "The Last Word: Great Commission: Ecclessiology", *Themelios*, Vol. 32, issue 3 April 2007, p. 68.

The Great Commission, especially the Matthew 28:18-20, is one of the most referred to and preached upon portions of Scripture by many Christians, especially those who engaged in missionary work, and the evangelical traditions. Some of them misunderstood or misinterpreted this with a conquering mood that it is "Christ's marching orders for the church" to "harvest pagan souls". Some think that it is a mandate given by Jesus to His disciples to "Christianize" the entire world or to extend the "Christendom" all over the world before His coming in glory.

One of the aims of this brief reflection will be to examine the Great Commission in order to expose some common erroneous usages of it and to determine its real meaning and significance for the church and the world today.

## 3. *EXTENSIO-DEI*[4]: A New Mission Paradigm to understand the Great Commission in Context

The popular interpretation of the great commission as per Matthew's gospel has given much emphasis for Jesus words of "sending" command, i.e., "go"... . It got the endorsement of the modern classical mission paradigm *Missio Dei. Missio Dei* anchored the concept and practice that the divine activity of sending, manifested through the sending of the Son by the Father and both the Father and the Son send the Spirit, and God the Trinity send the Church into the world. Hence, the *Missio-Dei* paradigm conceived the notion of biblical God as a 'sending' 'missionary' God.

The notion of 'sending' received high priority since the beginning of colonialism and the missionary institutions and individuals both Roman Catholics and Protestants. William Carey, the father of the modern protestant missionary movement, also considered Mt. 28:19-20 as the basic mission text[5].

*Missio Dei* with its emphasis on sending has given superiority complex among the thinkers and the practitioners of mission, both in the colonial period and today as well, which is from the centre to the periphery and from the powerful to the powerless. Chammah J. Kaunda and Roderick R. Hewitt endorse this in relation with the great commission saying:

> It was ideologically and theologically informed by Euro-centric thinking that adopted Matthew 28:18-20, the Great Commission paradigm to 'go, teach, baptise', as an imperative unidirectional framework of mission from the powerful to the powerless. Its practice became the implementation of the "Great Commission", that resulted in costly mis-

4 This new mission paradigm has recently introduced by the Roman Catholic Missiologist Jacob Kavunkal and for a detailed discussion on it See Jacob Kavunkal, A New Paradigm of Mission for Contemporary Times", *Ishvani Documenation and Mission Digest,* Vol. XXXII, No. 2, May – August. 2015

5 See, Jacob Kavunkal, "Extensio Dei...", p. 146.

> evangelisation and misrepresentation of Christ. Because it was primarily about saving souls to escape their context for another place, referred to as heaven. It consciously constituted a 'missiological alterity' by denigrating those who were perceived as not yet influenced by the Enlightenment to be 'uncivilized and primitive' and in need of enlightenment.[6]

Jacob Kavunkal also thinking in the same line and argues that the colonial mission theology was very much rooted in the spirit of the times, with its fascination with the new world across the seas, a world that was presumed to be of demons who took control of the souls whom the Lord Jesus Christ had purchased with His blood[7].

Vinayaraj also observes that the modern missionary movement bears the scars of its epistemological inclination with the colonial modernity[8]. This has been manifested in the missionary languages which have military connotations such as 'conquering nations for Christ' and the mood of cultural superiority that reflect in the terms referring third world people as 'barbarians, heathens, and animists'.

In this regard *Missio Dei* in relation with the great commission and its sending emphasis understood mission from the centre to the periphery, from the powerful to the powerless, and 'have' to the 'have-nots'. In contrast, we can understand mission also from the periphery to the centre, from the poor to the rich[9] which is the crux of ***Extensio Dei*** and this may lead us to have a better understanding of: Being Together: Fulfilling the Great Commission in Context.

### 3.1 *Extensio Dei*

Jacob Kavunkal opines that "Missio Dei refers chiefly to an activity of God, that of sending, where as the very nature of God is mission, reaching out"[10]. He argues that biblical narrative is not primarily a story of sending or of missions within a Trinitarian God and the Bible does not speak of a Trinitarian God, at least directly. Admittedly, we do have in the Bible instances of calling and sending including that of Jesus Christ; especially in the Johannine gospel and he calls us to remember that the church's mission began much before the doctrine of the Trinity has developed[11]. He reiterates that the Bible is the norm and foundation

6 Chammah J. Kaunda and Roderick R. Hewitt, "Together Towards Life": Reconceptualising *Missio*-Formation in Changing Landscape of World Christianity Pharos Journal of Theology ISSN 1018-9556 Vol. 96 - (2015) p. 5 http//: www.pharosjot.com (retrieved on 16 Oct. 2015).

7 Jacob Kavunkal, "Extensio Dei…", p. 146.

8 Yahu Vinayaraj Quoted in Chammah J. Kaunda and Roderick R. Hewitt, Together Towards Life…p. 5.

9 See, Jacob Kavunkal, "Extensio Dei…", p. 147.

10 Jacob Kavunkal, "Extensio Dei…", p. 147.

11 Ibid.

of all our discourse on mission and asking us to conform ourselves to the divine anthropology that we come across in the Bible, right from the beginning. He likes to encapsulate the entire biblical discourse in one pharse: Extensio Dei (*extendere* = to reach out), divine self-reaching out. For him, it is God's going out of God's self, in love. He described it as God's ecstasy – *ext stare*[12]. He describes:

> Humanly speaking, the first moment of this divine self-reaching out is creation. Creation is the manifestation of divine love, divine goodness. Hence the bible repeatedly asserts creation is good, and very good (Gen !:1-31... what is to be underlined is that God's reaching out to the world is not a second moment or an attribute of the divine being but just an expression of God's very being"[13].

God's divine self reaching out is depicted throughout the Bible in relation with the story of redemption, covenant, election and incarnation and also through the judges, prophets and ultimately through Jesus – the Word incarnate. A few examples: Gene. 3: 8, 9 (God reaches out Adam and Eve after they fall into sin), Gene.12:1-3 (Calling of Abraham), Exo. 3:1-10 (People of Israel at Egypt), Exo. 20. (Through covenant), Iss. 58:6-7, 61:1-2 (a God who reaches out His people), Matthew. 1:22, John. 1:14 (God with us) etc.

Walter Kasper points out that "God's being is present for his people and with his people"[14] and the scholars like Ulrich Wilkens opines that, "God's being is being-for-his-people: God's being as Pro-existence is the wonderful mystery of his existence"[15].

God's divine self reaching out continue throughout the human history and without any interruption or break it is continued in the mission and ministry of Jesus as Jacob Kavunkal points out: "It is God's work in the universe beginning with the ur-moment of creation. The Son proclaims and embodies God's liberating and healing action through the ushering in of the divine reign".[16] Thus the church's mission for Kavunkal is not just central to the understanding of God, it is the very nature and being of God which is seen as *Extensio Dei. Extensio Dei* unites the church with the life in God as well as life in the world in so far as the latter is ordained to be conformed to the divine reign of which the church is the sacrament. According to him the church derives its existence out of the process of this divine reaching out, as an ongoing continuation of the same. Thus the church's mission is seen in terms of its origin, God, and not in terms of its end,

12 Jacob Kavunkal, "Extensio Dei...", p. 148.

13 Ibid.

14 Walter Kasper, *Mercy: The Essence of the Gospel and the Key to Christian Life*, New York: Paulist Press, 20134, p. 48, also see, Jacob Kavunkal, "Extensio Dei...", p. 149.

15 Ulrich Wilkens quoted in Jacob Kavunkal, "Extensio Dei...", p. 149.

16 Jacob Kavunkal, "Extensio Dei...", p. 147. For a detailed discussion for this see pp. 150-52.

like places or followers of other faiths[17]. Hence, our mission is the mission of being the presence of God as reaching out the world, by living out the gospel that we have experienced in Jesus. This reminds us to do mission from the margins and not to the margins where they become powerful disciples to proclaim God's glory. "Marginalized people have God-given gifts that are under-utilized because of disempowerment and denial of access to opportunities and/or justice. Through struggles in and for life, marginalized people are reservoirs of the active hope, collective resistance, and perseverance that are needed to remain faithful to the promised reign of God"[18].

## 3.2 Make Disciples of All Nations: Mission as *Extensio Dei*

Many of the NT scholars are in the opinion that the word "go" (*poreúomai = to move from one place to another) is not the main directive in this Matthean great commission passage.* In Greek, the main action in Jesus commission words is *mathēteúō*, which is the Greek word translated "make disciples." Jesus assumes that the apostles will be going about. He tells them that, while they're going, they should make disciples. Hence the command here is **"as you go, make disciples"**.

Spiros Zodhiates, a renounced Greek scholar says about disciples: *Mathēteúō* means "to learn" and it is not only to learn, but to become attached to one's teacher and to become his follower in doctrine and conduct of life...that's pretty intense. But that's the kind of follower Jesus told his apostles to make[19]. Here being together with the master (Guru) is very important. In this regard, the great promise included in this great commission is poignant to note, "I am with you always, to the very end of the age". (Here, Matthew ends with the reassuring and empowering words of him who came to earth to be "God with us" Mtt. 1:23). Jesus is being with His disciples while they reach out the uttermost part of the world and entire creation. Hence, the mission of the church is the continuation of the incarnate Word, God's reaching out to the world and mission is where the Christian (Disciple) is. Making disciples "is primarily a matter of the Christian reaching out to the neighbor to realize the divine reign". In this regard, "we need to go beyond the divine sending and affirm mission as the very being of God and not just an activity and this invites every Christian to be missionary by reaching out to the neighbor. Christian existence is a constant self-transcendence through which a Christian makes the Transcendent God immanent"[20]. The church, as the communion of Christ's disciples, must become an inclusive community and exists to bring healing and reconciliation to the world. Last WCC reminds us

17 Jacob Kavunkal, "Extensio Dei...", p. 153.

18 "Together towards Life: Mission and Evangelism in Changing Landscapes", WCC, 2013, p. 16.

19 Jeffrey Kranz, "10 things I Wish Everyone to Know about Great Commission", www.faithstreet.com/ (retrieved on 23.10.2015).

20 Jacob Kavunkal, "Extensio Dei...", p. 155-56.

"Our participation in mission, our being in creation, and our practice of the life of the Spirit need to be woven together, for they are mutually transformative. We ought not to seek the one without the others. If we do, we will lapse into an individualistic spirituality that leads us to believe falsely that we can belong to God without belonging to our neighbour, and we will fall into a spirituality that simply makes us feel good while other parts of creation hurt and yearn"[21].

## 4. Hospitality: Fulfilling Great Commission in a Hostile and Pluralistic Society

When we hear 'hospitality' as a mission paradigm it may remind us of "rice Christians". It neither meant for producing rice Christians nor 'hospitality' is used as an enticement for conversion.

The word for hospitality is philexenos (Φιλόξενος) which means "loving the stranger (philos = loving and xenos = foreigner, stranger or outsider). The Bible both the Old Testament and the New Testament are highly commended on hospitality as a virtue e.g. Gen.18:1-15 and Mtth. 25:31-46. It is the natural outcome or character of a called out person or community by God in His grace and is the manifestation of glory and concern for the 'other'. The people of God are aliens and strangers whom God has welcomed into the "household of faith" (1Pet.2:9-10). So, the people of God in turn extend hospitality as making room for the stranger, not only in the community of faith but also in their neighborhood, especially those in acute needs. Hebrews 13:1–2: "Let brotherly love continue. Do not neglect to *show hospitality to strangers*, for thereby some have entertained angels unawares." So, love the brothers and sisters, but make sure that you don't neglect to love strangers as well.

Love for fellow Christians is important, essential — some call it "the final apologetic," based on John 13:35 — but there's a way in which it may not be all that impressive. Loving those who love you — "Do not even unbelievers do the same?" asks Jesus (Matthew 5:47). But showing love to outsiders, now that rings of life-change. That has the fingerprints of your heavenly Father all over it. Paul also reminds us "practice hospitality". Rom.12:13. (See also 1Timothy 3:2, and Titus 1:8). All these prove that hospitality is the inborn character of a disciple and it is vital in making disciples.

Christine D. Pohl who did an in-depth study on Biblical hospitality remind us that, loving care to the strangers must not be reduced to mere social entertainment nor may it be self-interested and reciprocal; instead, biblical hospitality reaches out to the abject and lowly and expects nothing in return. Hospitality is not optional, nor should it be understood as a rare spiritual gift; instead, it is a normative biblical practice that is **learned by doing it**. Hospitality is implicitly subversive in

21 "Together towards Life: Mission and Evangelism in Changing Landscapes", WCC, 2013, p. 10.

the way it shatters social boundaries, especially those boundaries enforced by table fellowship. When we eat with the lowly and welcome strangers and "sinners" to our table, we topple social expectations and bear witness to the kind of love God has for all his creatures[22]. Jesus is a role model in this regard and was accused that "He eats with tax collectors and sinners". Pohl reiterates that it was the radical nature of the Christian hospitality and a distinguished character of the early church which boosted the spreading of gospel, and helped them to overcome the social barriers that they encountered in the Greco-Roman world[23].

A disciple who is to make disciples of all nations should love the stranger, because we have been loved by the Master when we ourselves were strangers. Hospitality rises in its purest form when we heed Paul's counsel, "Remember that you were at that time separated from Christ, alienated from the commonwealth of Israel and *strangers* to the covenants of promise, having no hope and without God in the world" (Ephesians 2:12).

Hospitality accepts plurality and not keeps enmity in a hostile context or resist the violence with violence but diffuse the power to serve with even the cost of death. This is the way of Jesus showed on the last supper and asked us to continue till he come again in glory.

## 5. Conclusion

Disciple making teaches us to lean heavier on Jesus. Disciple making is not an easy task but a difficult work. When we become a disciple and we will see our weaknesses and failures and inadequacies like never before, and with God's help, it will teach us all the more to lean on Jesus. Being together with Jesus and His creation is the only way to fulfill the great commission in our present day context. Francis Pope reminds us "A true missionary, who never ceases to be a disciple, knows that Jesus walks with him, speaks to him, breaths with him, works with him. He senses Jesus alive with him in the midst of the missionary enterprise. Unless we see him present at the heart of our missionary commitment, our enthusiasm soon wanes and we are no longer sure of what it is that we are handing on; we lack vigour and passion. A person who is not convinced, enthusiastic, certain and in love, will convince nobody"[24]. Also the churches need to be on the move, journeying together in mission, continuing in the mission of the apostles. Practically, this

22 Christine D. Pohl, Making Room: Recovering Hospitality as a Christian Tradition, Eerdmans, 1999, p. 28ff. See also book review by David P. Gushee "Making Room: Recovering Hospitality as a Christian Tradition", Christian Ethics Today, Issue: 33, 2001, p. 21.

23 Christine D. Pohl, Making Room…p. 67.

24 Pope Francis, Apostolic Exortation, Evangeli Gaudium, the Joy of Gospel, Carmel International Publishing House, Trivandrum, 2013, p. 195.

means that church and mission should be united and that different ecclesial and missional bodies need to work together for the sake of life[25].

"We must be global Christians with a global vision because our God is a global God."

– John Stott

"Missionary zeal does not grow out of intellectual beliefs, nor out of theological arguments, but out of love"

– Roland Allen

25 "Together towards Life: Mission and Evangelism in Changing Landscapes", WCC, 2013, p. 40.

*Chapter 2*

# BIBLICAL UNDERSTANDING OF THE GREAT COMMISSION

Metropolitan Yuhanon Mor Meletius[1]

## 1. Introduction

In Hector Babenco movie "At Play with the Fields of the Lord", Wolf the Indian (played by Tom Waits), who got stranded in Mãe de Deus (meaning Mother of God in Portuguese) after his plane ran out of fuel, had a conversation in the local bar with Martin Quarrier (played by Aidan Quinn), a born again Christian Evangelist who came to spread the Christian gospel to the primitive Niaruna indigenous people. At the end of the conversation Wolf asked Quarrier, "The Lord made Indians the way they are, why you people make them different?"

I will come back to this a bit later. But for now, I am reminded of my good old days at UTC when professors would ask us to submit term papers and set a dead line. We will spend days and nights at the library and then in the room after 11 till the early hours of the following day to finish the paper. Finally, when it was over, would slip it through the front door of the concerned teacher's house just one minute before midnight of the dead line day. Then take a long sleep to wake up in the morning just before 8 am with enough time to wash our faces and brush our teeth, provided there was water in the tap, and also to escape the

1 HG Dr. Yuhanon Mor Meletius is the Metropolitan & Bishop of Malankara Orthodox Syrian Church.

frustration of having what Ramachandran in the kitchen called "uppuma", to go for the morning class.

I never thought I would have to go through the same drill all over again since I left UTC with my MTh certificate in 1984. However, now Rev. Dr. Santhosh S. Kumar called me back to go through the same process! On a serious note, I of course thank Dr. Santhosh for giving me this opportunity to be with you today and also for helping me do some serious study on the topic. I also thank Dr. Dexter S Maben for the generous introduction and for moderating this session.

There were several challenges before me. First of all, a bishop in normal case doesn't do this sort of things. When I visited UTC in March 1991 few months after I was consecrated a bishop, Dr. E. C. John, then Principal, introduced me to the community in the Chapel after the morning worship. I replied to his hearty welcome saying, "I am happy to introduce myself as a successful pastor after having received the training at UTC, or should I say a successful politician after having spent six long years in UTC campus. I was elected to the office when I was in US doing my graduate studies at Lutheran School of Theology at Chicago (LSTC) and hence was absent in India where the election was held." You got the point, I suppose. We bishops seldom do brain storming, but do remote manuring quite well. Now Dr. Santhosh has done it back on me, a term paper through remote control. It is really hard to do such a thing in my kind of job.

Again I am a Hebrew Scripture student and haven't done any serious work on a New Testament passage lately. The most recent one was "A Sociological Study of the Book of Revelations" done for Prof. Dr. David Rhoads at LSTC in 1990. You can imagine how poorly equipped I am to deal with a serious topic like **"The Great Commission: Biblical Perspective"!**

Further, the volume of literature produced on the subject is so much and to make a select bibliography itself is a Herculean task. Finally, to get the right ones at hand in Thrissur where I live was also not that easy. I stated all these, to make an anticipatory bail plea. I don't think I have done justice to the subject in this paper, but I have tried to raise a few questions in relation to the subject that I think are important in the given socio-political situation in our country.

We live in a world that is constantly evolving. In the process, the challenges posed are quite significant considering the fact that any evolution in the created world should take God's creation to the ultimate goal of freeing it from all slavish and oppressive situations. It is to fulfil this goal that we are asked to "go". This imperative comes from none other than the creator of "all the nations" Himself (cf. John 1:3) who has chosen to 'go' in front as a model, as a guide, as a participant, as a herald and as one who empowers. He Himself walked that path first and then has passed the baton to His disciples for them to walk it further. He has also shown them how to walk that road.

Time moves forward in clockwise mode. We cannot go backward at any cost. The challenges are new and hence the need to revise the methodology to make it relevant and 'current' always. Those were times when people accepted and believed things as it appeared to be or were told to be. People call it pre-scientific days or pre-modern era. In such times, the powerful and the educated had their time and say. But then came the modern era with the backdrop of renaissance and industrial revolution. People took the liberty to ask questions. But still a lot of things were accepted as they were explained by others. The one who said, 'earth is a globe', had to submit an apology for saying what he saw through the lens of his telescope. But then came post-modern age where every corner of the whole socio-cultural arena was put to question. They talked about de-construction of multiple voices, rejection of meta-narratives which said, 'truth is relative' and rejected the absolute and ultimate claims of reason. This put the emphasis on the reader instead of on the text itself. Further, that age gave way to what is called as 'pseudo-modern' era. According to Alan Kirby, this age is marked by, 'phones, clicks, presses, surfs, chooses and moves'.[2] We are now brought to this current world to which Christ asks us to "go". It becomes our responsibility to analyse, study and make viable methodology to 'go', 'make disciples', 'baptize' and 'teach'.

## 2. The Great Commission

No one knows for sure who actually named this passage "The Great Commission". However, it is generally considered that a Dutch missionary by name Justinian von Welz (1621-88) first coined the phrase and later Hudson Taylor (1832-1905) made it popular.[3] People like Edward Riggenbach ("Trinitarische Taufbefehl" - 1903) and J. H. Oldham, et. al. ("The Missionary Motive" - 1913) 'asserts that this concept did not exist until after 1650. Traditionally, it was considered as a commission directed to the first audience of 500 only and never thought of having continued relevance.[4]

Even though there are five commissioning passages in the New Testament (Matthew 28: 16-20; Mark 16:14-18; Luke 24:36-49; John 20:19-23 and Act. 1:6-8) the one in Matthew which is called "The Great Commission" will be the passage for our consideration. Questions have been raised about the authenticity of this passage to the effect that doubts its validity whether this was exactly what Jesus told his disciples or not. R. Funk suggests, "These commissions have little in common, which indicates that they have been created by the individual evangelists to express their conception of the future of the Jesus movement. As a consequence

2 Alan Kirby, "The Death of Post-Modernism and Beyond," *Philosophy Now: A Magazine of Ideas.*, no. Oct-Nov (2015). https://philosophynow.org/issues/58/The_Death_of_Postmodernism_And_Beyond.

3 Robbie F. Castleman, "The Last Word: The Great Commission: Ecclesiology," *Themelios* 32, no. 3 (2007), p. 68

4 "Great Commission", Wikipedia: The Free Encyclopedia; (Wikimedia Foundation Inc., https://en.wikipedia.org/wiki/Great_Commission (accessed on 20 October 2015).

they cannot be traced back to Jesus"[5]. To Hubbard, 'even the proto-commission on which all the commission passages were based did not come from Jesus'.[6] There are also people who consider it as coming from 'post-Jesus theological statements'.[7] FF Bruce concludes, "Matthew's record of the commission is unique and cannot be compared with any other record of the post-resurrection appearance of Jesus"[8]. To Hal Freeman, "It only tells us that Jesus wanted his disciples to continue the mission he began".[9] The writers of the Gospel of Matthew commentary affirm, "Through these words, Mathew looks forward to the continuing work of the Messianic Community, making it explicit what has already been hinted elsewhere about a mission to those outside the Old Covenant community, Israel".[10] As far as we are concerned, it is enough to say that this is Matthew's version of what Jesus wanted His disciples to do after His ascension and hence has to be taken seriously.

According to Matthew, Galilee was the location of the event. Jesus started His ministry in Galilee (Matt. 4:15) and the end also happens there. In Mark no precise geographical location is given. It only says, that the event happened inside a house and they were dining (Mk. 16:14ff.). For Luke they were in Jerusalem in a house and many were there in a perplexed mood (Luke 24:33ff.). Jesus appeared to them while those who returned from Emmaus were narrating their experience with the Lord before others including the eleven and "those who were with them". Then Jesus led 'them' to Bethany and was lifted up. In John again it did not happen in a mountain. The 'mountain' in Matthew suggests that Jesus was higher in status than Moses, a theme Mathew had already introduced.[11] But to Grand, the mountain points to "a place of divine revelation" and has nothing to do with Moses.[12]

---

5 Robert W., et al. Funk, *The Five Gospels: The Search for the Authentic Words of Jesus: New Translation and Commentary* (San Francisco: Harper Collings, 1997), p. 270.

6 B. Hubbard, *The Matthean Redaction of a Primitive Apostolic Commissioning: An Exegesis of Matthew 28:16-20* (Missoula: Scholars Press, 1974), pp. 116-128.

7 J. Meier, "Two Disputed Questions in Matt 28:16-20," *Journal of Biblical Literature* 96, no. 3 (1977), pp. 422-424.

8 Frederick F. Bruce, "The End of the First Gospel," *The Evangelical Quarterly* 12, (1940), p. 204.

9 Hal Freeman, "The Great Commission and the New Testament: An Exegesis of Matthew 28:16-20," *Southern Baptist Journal of Theology* 1:4, no. Winter (1997), p. 15.

10 William F. Albright, ed. *The Anchor Bible. Matthew: A New Translation with Introduction and Commentary*, ed. C. S. Mann, Vol. 26 (Garden City. New York: Doubleday & Company. Inc., 1979), p. 361.

11 Robert Gundry, Matthew: A Commentary on His Handbook for a Mixed Church Under Persecution. Grand Rapids, MI: William B. Eerdmans Publishing Company, (1994), pp. 593-594.

12 Grand R. Osborne, "Redaction Criticism and the Great Commission: A Case Study toward a Biblical Understanding of Inerrancy" *JETS* 19/2, no. Spring (1976), pp. 76-77.

The number of people present at the event varies in the Gospels. In Matthew and Mark only 11 were present. In Luke the number is not limited as there were the eleven with those who returned from Emmaus along with 'those others'. In John it is not clear who all were there. All that we can say is, the word 'disciple' in John may imply many more than ten apostles (Thomas was not present at that moment and Judas had died). Acts talks about "they" without specifying the number. Lenski thinks that the number was larger than eleven as those 'doubted' cannot be those worshipped'.[13] He quotes 1 Cor. 15:6 to support his point. But Matthew doesn't give us any room for guesswork about the number as he says "Now the eleven disciples went to Galilee" (v.16).

It is quite clear in Matthew that there were no women present during the "Great Commission". But Luke certainly thought women were also there when Jesus commissioned. As already seen, John does not give definite number leaving space for doubt. Even though, according to Matthew, women were not present during the event he narrates at the mountain, their role as commissioned disciples cannot be ignored. They were the ones who first received commission to take the news of the Lord's resurrection to the disciples from the Lord Himself (Matt. 28:8-10. It should also be noted that when the women saw Jesus they did not doubt as the disciples did but only 'took hold of His feet and worshipped Him'!). A Boyd Luter Jr.,[14] after a detailed exegetical study of all the five commission passages concludes that "By now, it should be sufficiently clear from the exegetical/ literary angles discussed that such women as Mary, the mother of Jesus, Mary Magdalene, Salome, a number of unnamed women at the Cross (Mark 15:41; Luke 23:49, 55), as well as others like Joanna and Susanna (Luke 8:1-3), should all be considered as much full-fledged disciples as the eleven." He affirms, "Though often painted in somewhat subtle literary hues, their commitment as disciples (Luke 14:26-33) of the Lord Jesus does shine through and should be emulated by growing disciples today".[15]

Though the passage from verses 16-20 is called "the Great Commission", actual commission is in verses 19-20a. Verse 16 talks about the geographical location; verse 17 is about the response of the disciples at the sight of Jesus and in v. 18 Jesus' authority statement is given. Verse 20b gives Jesus' assurance of His presence with the disciples.

## 3. "As You Go" or "Go"

There has been quite a lot of discussion in the scholarly world with regard to the grammatical structure of the passage. The first verb πορευθέντες (*Poreutentes* - go)

13 Culver Lenski, "Commentary: The Book of Matthew," *JETS* 10/2, no. Spring (1967), p. 555.

14 A. Boyd Luter Jr., "Women Disciples and the Great Commission," *Trinity Journal* 16:2, no. Fall (1995), p. 185.

15 Ibid.

is an aorist participle. The other verbs - *μαθητεύσατε (matheteusate of matheteuo-* make disciples) is an aorist imperative, *βαπτιζοντες (baptizontes* - baptize) and *διδάσκοντες* (*didaskontes* - teach) are present nominative plural participles. There are two opinions about the way we should translate the aorist imperative and aorist participle verbs in the sentence and about their mutual relationship.[16]

Robert D. Culver argues that the first verb *poreutentes* has to be translated as "as ye go ..." to mean "where ever you may go...".[17] Whereas Nigel Turner,[18] would argue that even though, in general case, the participle verb will not have a standing by itself, here in this case the context decides the meaning. Hence, the verb 'go' has to be given an imperative tone to say "go and ..." There are several examples in Matthew that would support this argument. In Matt. 2:8a where "go and search..." is preferred instead of 'when you go, search out ...'. In Matt. 2:20 ("Rise take the child..."); in 5:24 ("come and offer...) and in many other occasions (see 6:6; 11:4; 17:221:27; 28:7 etc.) this principle is followed in translating the text. If we take Culver's argument, it will make the going 'optional' and since there was no earlier direction to go, making of disciples will become optional and consequently 'no great commission' in effect.

Cleon quotes (p. 261), Adolf Schlatter whose opinion he thinks right as, "When two actions are connected with one process, the aorist participle which prepares for the actions is placed before the aorist of the main verb. This sentence structure occurs so often in Matthew that it characterizes the style of Matthew."[19] For Cleon, Matthew got this style from the Septuagint where aorist participle verb can carry the weight of aorist imperative when the other verb is imperative.[20] So it is well on our part to conclude that the direction is to "go ... and make disciples..." Without the going, the making of disciples is not possible, and especially when "all nations" is the object".[21] It cannot be a casual act as suggested by the translation "as you go..."

## 4. Who Doubted?

Further on the question of 'doubt', K. Grayston argues that the answer to this question depends of how *hoi de* is translated. According to him, a similar case

---

16 Cleon Rogers, "The Great Commission," *BSAC* 130:519, no. July (1973), pp. 258-259.

17 D. Culver, "What Is the Church's Commission? Some Exegetical Issues in Matthew 28:16-20," *Bibliotheca Sacra* CXXV, no. July- September (1968), p. 253.
See also Roy B Zuck, "Greek Words for Teach," *Bibliotheca Sacra* CXXI, no. April-June (1965), p. 163.

18 James Hope and et al Moulton, *Syntax" Vol. III. A Grammar of New Testament Greek* (Edinburgh: T & T Clark, 1963).

19 Schlatter. Adolph, *Der Evangelist Matthäus* (Stuttgart: 1948), p. 23.

20 Ibid., p. 260-262.

21 Ibid., p. 260.

is seen in Matthew 2:5 where *hoi de* is not translated in a "partisan style".[22] L. Morris says, "It can scarcely mean that the hesitaters were among the worshipers; Matthew is saying that there were those who worshiped and there were those who hesitated."[23] But, Don Fanning contents that the 'verb distaze can mean waver or be of two minds.'[24] Ellis argues that, 'Matthew wanted to express the mixed feelings of the eleven and there was no need for more people.'[25] The use of the term *distaze* in Matt. 14:31 ("Oh man of little faith why did you doubt?") supports this argument. To C. H. Dodd, 'doubt is only the sign of seeking further assurance that Jesus is truly resurrected'.[26] As said earlier, it is to be said that since Matthew has a clear statement about the number of people who went to Galilee to receive the commission and to receive the assurance of Jesus' continued presence with (v.15), we have no other option but accept the fact that there were only eleven present at the time of "the Great Commission."

## 5. Authority

In his statement on Matt 28:18, Albright suggests that the phrase *pasa exousia en ourano* (all authority is given to me in heaven) seems to be a reflection of what we see in Dan. 7:14 in line with the powers of the "Son of Man".[27] But, we do not see any sign of vengeance in this passage as seen in Daniel. Robert Gundry rules out the possibility of any relation between Matthew's statement and what we see in the Daniel passage.[28] Jesus through this statement provided confidence in the mind of the disciples that they didn't have to be perplexed or confused, but be assured that He was the one who had power over them and also over those whom they will meet when they go.

The statements about His authority in the beginning and the assurance of His presence at the end are well placed on either side of His commission to go, make disciples, baptize and teach. This makes the proclamation even more fruitful and effective.[29] We have already seen that the verb "go", though an aorist participle, is to be taken as the primary command from Jesus. However, the aorist imperative

---

22 Grayston, "The Translation of Matthew 28.17," *Journal for the Study of the New Testament* 21, (1984), p. 105.
See also R. Kwik, "Some Doubted," *Expository Times* 77, (1965-66). p. 181.

23 L. Morris, *The Gospel According to Matthew* (Grand Rapids, MI: William B. Eerdmans Publishing Company, 1992), p. 745.

24 Don Fanning, "The Great Commission," *JLBTS* 1:2 no. Article 2 (2014), p. 3.

25 I. P. Ellis, "But Some Doubted," *New Testament Studies* 14, (1967-68), p. 576.

26 C. H. Dodd, "The Appearances of the Risen Christ: An Essay in Form Criticism," in *More New Testament Studies* (London: 1968), p. 12.

27 Albright, ed. p. 362.

28 Robert Gundry, p. 595. See also H. M. Teeple, "The Origin of the Son of Man Christology," *JBL*, Sept, (1965).

29 Fanning, "The Great Commission." p. 4 .

verb "make disciples' also has to be given equal weight since both are inseparably linked. The meaning implied becomes go (with an implied urgency of the aorist imperative) and immediately begin to make disciples of all nations.[30]

## 6. Make Disciples

The phrase "make disciple" (*Μαθητευω - matheteno*) is essentially a Matthean phrase. According to Matt. 13:52 a disciple is the one who has been trained. Matt. 27:57 talks about Joseph of Arimathea as a disciple. Hence for Mathew, a disciple is to be both trained and has to follow the master. A relevant question at this point would be, has discipleship got anything to do with becoming a member of a denomination? All along the history of the Church, in most cases, denominations have been baptizing and making disciples as if disciples should, by virtue of it, become member of an organized Church or denomination. Of course, disciple will always seek a community for fellowship. But, the question whether the nature of that fellowship need to be like that of an established denomination is crucial.

The literal meaning of the word baptize is 'dyeing' (a cloth). But, here the verb is used to describe the "act of initiation into the Messianic Community".[31] One who is baptized gets a new colour, that of the Triune God, the Father, the Son and the Holy Spirit. "Mathew believed that Jesus' unique status with the Father was essential to the mission. Thus, the passage is both Christological and missiological"[32]

## 7. The Trinitarian Formula

Questions have been raised regarding the Trinitarian formula used in the passage. Lack of this formula in the Book of Acts when baptism is referred to raises doubts about its authenticity. J. Schaberg is of the opinion that 'this formula was introduced in to the community only after Jesus.'[33] Even what is said of the Spirit in Romans 8:9-11 cannot be taken as proof for its early use either.[34] But it has to be remembered that this phrase cannot be considered as very late since we have reference to it in Didache 7:1-3. Albright argues that "This formula doesn't need to be seen as retrojected in to the text from post-Nicene orthodoxy as the concept

30 Wallace Arthur Alcon, "The Great Commission: Disciples. Basic Greek Grammar," *CENQ* 2:4, no. Winter (1959), p. 645.

31 Albright, ed. p. 362.

32 Freeman, "The Great Commission and the New Testament: An Exegesis of Matthew 28:16-20", p. 19.

33 J. Schaberg, *The Father, the Son, and the Holy Spirit: The Triadic Phrase in Matthew 28:19b* (Chico, CA: Scholars Press, 1980), pp. 9, 14, 24–26.

34 Gordon D. Fee, ed. *Christology and Pneumatology in Romans 8:9-11* (Grand Rapids, MI: William B. Eerdmans Publishing Company, 1996). Also see Joel B and Max Turner Green, ed. *Elsewhere: Some Reflections on Paul as a Trinitarian," Jesus of Nazareth: Lord and Christ* (Grand Rapids, MI: William B. Eerdmans Publishing Company, 1994), pp. 312-331.

of God as Father, Son and Holy Spirit is as old as the Messianic community."[35] He further states that "even if it is not taken as a liturgical formula, which is a later one, it could be seen as what baptism accomplished, fellowship and participation with the Messianic community."[36] According to FF Bruce,[37] The textual evidence for the words "baptizing them… Holy Ghost" is quite remarkable. All the available manuscripts and version have this formula. Only Eusebius among the Christian Fathers has mentioned one without. It is doubtful whether we can trust that over against all the other testimonies. To John McKenzie, "The Trinitarian formula in the baptism in Matthew "represents a more mature practice."[38] He further states that there is no mention of baptism but 'in the name of' and 'all nations' are only present in Luke 24:47 which was taken by Eusebius as proof.[39] He continues to say that, 'though these three persons are not mentioned together in Matthew, we have Father and Son in Matt. 11:27 and Son and Holy Spirit in Matt. 12:32.'[40] Bruce concludes: "This particular usage is relevant to the Gentile converts. The words of Matthew xxviii are concerned with Gentiles, those without the knowledge of God, who had to learn what Jews knew already of the God of revelation, as well as the Good News of the New Covenant. They, therefore, are to be baptized "into the name of the Father and of the Son and of the Holy Ghost"; and the universal Church has acted rightly in using the full Trinitarian formula in the rite of baptism."[41] As far as we are concerned, beyond the precise way a particular Christian community may understand and practice baptism, it should refer to a thorough washing and filling as Jesus told Nicodemus in John 2:22. By these two, a steady and continuous change to the better of a person and communities is implied. Baptism, like any other act in Christ's community cannot be a onetime event; rather an event started at a given point of time and continues eternally renewing the effect and purpose.

## 8. All Nations

The phrase *panta ta ethne* (all the nations) brings a universalistic goal to the mission. Hare and Harrington have raised question about whether this would include Jews

---

35 Albright, ed. p. 362. He quotes Biblical passages like 1Cor. 12:4-6; 2 Cor.13:14; 1 Pet. 1:2; 1 John 3:23-24 to establish his point.

36 Ibid., p. 363.

37 Bruce, "The End of the First Gospel", p. 204.

38 John L. McKenzie, "The Gospel According to Matthew," in *The Jerome Biblical Commentary Ii: The New Testament and Topical Articles*, ed. Raymond E. Brown and others (Bangalore: St. Peter's Seminary, 1972), p. 114.

39 Bruce, "The End of the First Gospel", p. 204.

40 Ibid.

41 Ibid., pp. 205-206.

or not.[42] To them *ethnos* and *ethne* always mean "gentile/s" in Matthew. They think that Gospel according to Matthew was written after Christians parted with Jews.[43] This was questioned by J. Miller to whom, Mathew may have never thought that the mission for Jews had ended.[44] At least that is not the impression we get from Matthew 10:23. To Hal Freeman, what Matthew means is "conversion has to be keeping the ethnic identity intact."[45]

## 9. Teaching

Boyd Luter comments that 'teaching' the baptized disciples "is for them to grow through obedience to the Lord's standards."[46] In the Rabbinical teaching context the teacher and the student enter into a close fellowship with each other. The students would submit completely to the teacher and would follow him where ever he would go. The submission and devotion of the students to the teacher is phenomenal. The students will be at the service of the teacher always and even the relation to the father and mother would come only next to this.[47] Jesus was "a good teacher" in the eyes of many and particularly to his close followers (Matt. 8:19; 12:38; 19:16; 22:16, 24, 36). The question is, was Jesus asking his disciples to bring those who were baptized to the same level of the disciples themselves? When we compare the two words disciples (v. 16) and teaching (v. 20), this is the conclusion we can derive at.

"The present tense "to observe" (*τηρειν*, "to be keeping, observing, fulfilling") indicates that the teaching must involve not just what is taught but also the resultant life-long committal to obey the message. The Christian teaching being imparted is expected henceforth to control and mould the entire life and character of the believer."[48] What Jesus commanded can be seen in Matthew 5. On the one hand, a correction of what has been taught in the past and on the other what is to be done in and through the new community (5:21-48). We may also consider the content of Jesus' first message in the Synagogue in Nazareth (Luke 4:18-19) in this context.

Teaching also should involve teaching of the ways of the world, its influence and how to face those challenges in the world (John 17:15). There is a radical demand for a changed life. "*Panta* would therefore refer to the totality of Jesus'

42 D. and D. Harrington Hare, "Make Disciples of All the Nations," *CBQ* 37, (1975), pp. 359-369.

43 Ibid., p. 363.

44 J. Miller, "Nations or Gentiles in Matthew 28:19?," *CBQ* 39, (1977), pp. 94-102.

45 Freeman, "The Great Commission and the New Testament: An Exegesis of Matthew 28:16-20", p. 18.

46 Luter Jr., "Women Disciples and the Great Commission", p. 174.

47 Rogers, "The Great Commission", p. 262.

48 D. Edmond Hiebert, "An Expository Study of Matthew 28:16-20," *BSAC* 149/595, no. July (1992), p. 352.

teaching, especially as presented in the first gospel, centring on the coming kingdom of heaven and man's relation to it as well as on the Person of Jesus".[49] In the present socio-political atmosphere emerging in our country with the neo-colonial tendencies, divination of market and corporate enthusiasm with a culture of greed in the loose, people need to be taught of self-esteem, freedom and self-respect which are given by God in creation. God asked Moses to bring people out of Egypt not because they had no better life there (Ex. 16:3), but because they did not know God and were not free to know. Relation to God decides the identity of human. They were not as much slave to Pharaoh as to the deprivation of knowing God and relating to Him in worship.

## 10. Until the Close of Ages

The commission ends with Jesus' promise of his presence with the disciples "until the close of ages" and that makes the end of the Gospel also. We have a fitting conclusion with an assurance not only for those who were with him, but for all generations to come. This assurance certainly agrees with the name 'Immanuel' which Matthew gave Jesus at the very beginning of the Gospel.[50] The phrase "To the end of the ages" represents an old sectarian formula that testifies to the fact that the passage belongs to the earliest stages of the tradition.[51]

We might raise a question whether the presence of Christ is 'with the Church' or with 'those who follow the commandments'. It all depends on what a Church is. Church basically has to be people who follow the path of Christ rather than an established and structured organization, unless that organization becomes true to its calling and creates a true fellowship of disciples of Jesus transcending all barriers and discriminative tendencies.

The continuing presence of Jesus with the disciples made them share the authority Jesus was talking about at the beginning of the commissioning. That is why Peter and John were able to say, "in the name of Jesus Christ of Nazareth", to the question from the Sanhedrin "By what power, or in what name did you do this" when they had healed a lame man (Acts 4:7ff.). This is why Bruce commented, "The commission was no 'dead letter' to them, but in fact with life-giving spirit! Not only had they His authority, but His very presence."[52]

---

49 Osborne, "Redaction Criticism and the Great Commission: A Case Study Toward a Biblical Understanding of Inerrancy", p. 81.

50 Albright, ed. p. 363. Matt. 1:23. Also 18:20.

51 Ibid.

52 Bruce, "The End of the First Gospel", p. 211.

## 11. Few Further Observations

Being a student of Hebrew Scripture, I should also look in to the past history of God and His works with His people to find if something similar can be seen there.

What happened in the Garden of Eden was not seen by God as an act against God only. It was also seen as an act against the identity and integrity of nature and everything in it (Gen. 2:15). God saw the aggression against the fruit of a tree so grave a matter that he had to pronounce that relationship of human with God, with nature and with humans were affected adversely by that act (I do not see the passage in Gen. 3:24 the way it has been interpreted traditionally as God casting human out of the Garden. On the contrary, God was just pronouncing the effect of human conduct). This should tell us about how God would be looking at our ecological miss-management and our ill-treating of nature which was entrusted upon humans to 'keep and cultivate'. It was the lack of readiness on the part of humans to participate with God in His attempt to make the seventh day effect ever and everlasting.

To re-establish the broken relationship, humans had to be brought in to fellowship with God first. God who has been working in the history of His creation always sought the participation of humans to re-establish the broken relationship between God and human and between human and everything else including fellow humans. God's readiness to take participation of humans in the life of everything else is displayed through God bringing all animals He made before human to be named (Gen. 2:19). Even after the fall, God did not give up on that. This is what we see in the calling of Abraham and asking him to go that he may become a blessing to all (Gen. 12: 3b - "... and in you all families of the earth will be blessed". Also see 46:1-5a). C. Westermann finds a pattern in God's involvement in the life of people.[53] The promise Abraham received was carried through to the future history of Israel. It was this presence that sheltered and accompanied Abraham and which continued through the period of monarchy in Israel, and beyond this closed community, hoped to be extended to all the families of the earth.[54] Incarnation was necessitated as the children of Abraham too failed in carrying out the mission entrusted. Now the call comes again to those who followed the 'Immanuel'.

---

53 Claus Westermann, *Genesis 12-36: A Commentary.*, ed. John J. Scullion, Vol. 2 (Minneapolis: Augsburg Publishing House, 1985), pp. 146-147 (I am skipping everything narrated in terms of mission entrusting in the patriarchal history for brevity of the presentation).

54 Ibid., p. 147.

When Abraham was called he was commanded to abandon radically his natural roots and to go to an unknown world.[55] Abraham was assigned the role of a mediator of blessing in God's saving plan for all the families of the earth.[56]

The verb "go" has the implication of self-denial. "To belong to the apostolic community is to be involved in the complex act of giving away, to be at the disposal of God's will, to give away the life which we have, so that God's life can be given through us."[57] "It cannot be said that the Church has a mission of salvation to fulfil in the world. It is the mission of the Trinity that invites the Church to participate in."[58]

The nature of the commission to "go" entrusted with the disciples of Jesus carries the same command as that given to Abraham. Paul exhorts his readers to follow the model of Jesus' in self-emptying (Phil. 2:5-8). This is what we see in the making of a disciple who received the commission. Leave aside everything that is supposed to be holding them back. Kenosis, used often in the Christian thought circles need to be what is seen here. The disciple has to leave even the pride of being a disciple. A Christian has to leave the 'Christian pride' in that person. In the Indian context even the claims of minority rights need to be given up. There shall not be any special privilege claim, except that of a citizen of the country that is offered and open to everyone else, to become a witnessing community in this ancient culture.[59]

"Immanuel" was the message that came from God to His creation. Authority is not a theory. It becomes effective only in participation. God's authority was and continues to be displayed in creation and salvation. Both were combined in Christ event as a new creation was made and a new liberative act was performed.

Christ's authority over the people in their need was not effectively displayed when Jesus went to His home town (Mark 6:1-6). Even with Jesus' claim of all authority He was given, still our lack of participation with Him and with one another will make that authority ineffective. Hence, our participation with humans and nature is the only way, as his disciples, through which we can make the authority of Jesus working in and through. This calls us for a participatory life style in going out, making disciples and teaching. The Trinitarian formula becomes a model for our participation. Father, Son and Holy Spirit are together and in participation bring about transformation in a person. So, being baptized

55 Gerhard von Rad, *Genesis: A Commentary. Otl* (Philadelphia: The Westminster Press, 1973), p. 159.

56 Ibid., p. 160.

57 R. Williams, *Open to Judgement* (London: DLT, 1994), p. 257.

58 Lynne J. Wall, "The Great Commission: Biblical Perspective" www.methodist.org.nzp. Quoted from Jurgen Moltmann on the difference between 1910 and 2010 World Missionary Conferences.

59 Of course this doesn't mean that those privileges offered by the constitution to Dalits, Tribes and economically backward communities are to be disregarded.

in the name of the Father, of the Son and of the Holy Spirit creates a binding effect on each disciple to the fellow being after the model seen in the mutual relationship between the three persons in the Holy Trinity. Jesus' words "I and my Father are one" (John 10:30), "I know that you hear me always" (John 11:42), etc. talk about a participatory kind of relationship between the Father and the Son. Again Jesus talked clearly about the relationship between the Father, the Son and the Spirit of Truth (John 14 and16). Same should happen in the mission of Jesus' disciples today, I believe.

In and through participation, everyone and everything around us should reflect Christ's mission model/style. Participate with everyone to create a world that is of God where everyone can live and grow in peace and harmony. Jesus is calling His disciples to make 'the Nazareth Manifesto' our own manifesto in the mission He has entrusted with us. I earnestly and sincerely think that the "Great Commission" is all about this. We are commissioned to involve ourselves in the struggle of others, even risking our own safety, in making their lives better in terms of quality and identity. To Rev Jeevan Babu, "Mission is not what we want to do. Mission is what others expect from us. Mission is relational and not one sided. Therefore, mission should be other-oriented, commitment-oriented, call-oriented and pro-life oriented. The questions of children, especially children deprived of basic education but have to work in factories and other sectors, women who are deprived of freedom and womanhood, the outcasts, poor and the marginalized are to be our concern."[60] We are called to "go" and participate with these ones in their struggle for a life with quality, identity, self-respect and freedom.

Effective participation can happen only if there is mutual understanding. Mutual knowing can happen only through dialogue. As renowned ecumenist M. M. Thomas has pointed out, 'we cannot ever say that one culture is superior to another since we live in a culturally pluralistic world but each need to become better in some way or other.[61] We need to approach the other without prejudice and any kind of superiority complex, but as God's gift to the created world.

Discipling has gone through several stages in the past, says Anthoniraj Tumma.[62] Tumma lists the stages as given by Raymond Panikkar. They are, witness (until Avius), conversion (until the impact of Islam), crusade (until the discovery of America) and Mission (until the end of the colonial era). To Panikkar today is the time of dialogue.[63] Dialogue helps understand each other with their myths, cultures and concepts. Even the understanding of God and God's ways of working can only be understood through dialogue. In the movie, I mentioned earlier, there is a reference to the name Jesus as understood by the people of the land as a deity

60 Jeevan Babu, *Mission Hermeneutics: Ncci Resource Series* (Nagpur: 1996.), p. 2.

61 M. M. Thomas, *Some Theological Dialogue* (Madras: CISRS & CLS, 1977), p. 140ff.

62 Anthoniraj Tumma, *Breaking Barriers: Liberation of Dialogue and Dialogue of Liberation, The Quest of R. Panikkar and Beyond* (Delhi: ISPCK, 2000).

63 Ibid., p. 4.

of death. Without understanding each other no discipleship is possible in the Indian context (same should be the case in any other given context).

Jesus who was able to work effectively and freely across various communities in and around the geographical area of his ministry is calling us, without judging or condemning any of the cultures and communities around us, to go and make disciples, not to increase the number in a particular denomination or a group, but to teach them the ways of Jesus, the way of involvement in the life of the other in order to liberate them from bondage and to help them transform or to be baptized and to be taught. Here, the whole idea of 'baptising' gets a new meaning. It is not adding people to a denomination or a different group, but to help them become transformed, wherever they may be.

The world is evolving and we are to be on the move because we were asked to "go". "No part of any culture can continue unchanged; all elements of a culture must be re-patterned in the light of the demand of Christ, to enable them to express the message of Christ, and the dignity and justice conferred on men (human) by Christ."[64] The call is to "go" to all nations to make disciples. Here we need to take the context where Jesus grew up in Galilee which had a mixed ethnic population and people were more open without any exclusivist or extremist attitude. This pluralistic society may have had quite an influence on Jesus.[65] This was a model atmosphere for Jesus to consider when He coined His mission statement for all peoples. So, when disciples of Jesus, then or in the present day situation we, are asked to go out to present what Jesus taught among the peoples, it is not for us to change the way they live their life, but help them grow in their own environment as God's children. Hence, we need to take seriously the cultural context existing in each given society without changing or judging it as pagan or satanic, but proclaiming only the Gospel. It is in this context the question presented by Wolf of the movie, which I talked about in the beginning, becomes relevant, "The Lord made Indians the way they are, why you people make them different?" Michael Patton, who writes on "Representing Christ to the Postmodern World",[66] concludes his article by saying, "We understand that tolerance is a mandate within the Church. We also understand that the Bible teaches that there are many situations in which truth is relative."[67] This approach is vital to the effectiveness of our going and making disciples in the postmodern or pseudo-modern world.

---

64 Thomas., p. 147.

65 Albright, ed. p. 359, 362 Cf. "Galilee of the nations" in Isa. 8:23.

66 Michael Patton, "Representing Christ to a Postmodern World" https://bible.org/article/representing-christ-postmodern-world (accessed on Oct 2015).

67 Ibid.

## 12. Conclusion

Jesus initiated a mission, a mission to bring God's message of "the year of God's favour" to all creatures. Of course that was a mission that God started at the very beginning. Jesus worked out that mission through His life, death and resurrection. He proved on Himself beyond doubt that he had authority over everything, even upon death. That was a strong message to everyone and hence there should be no hurdle in this world that cannot be faced with Him to make things better and perfect. His name is 'Immanuel' and hence His empowering presence is assured. He has commissioned His disciples to take this initiated message of outliving 'to all nations' by 'going' and 'making disciples.' He has entrusted with those who have already got that message to invite on His behalf every people and cultures to be taught. His disciples are called to "go" to involve and participate in the life of people and cultures to transform it that it shall become "baptized" and "taught" so that they be made "disciples".

## Bibliography


"Great Commission", Wikipedia: The Free Encyclopedia; (Wikimedia Foundation Inc., https://en.wikipedia.org/wiki/Great_Commission (accessed on 20 October 2015).

Adolph, Schlatter. *Der Evangelist Matthäus*. Stuttgart, 1948.

Albright, William F. ed. *The Anchor Bible. Matthew: A New Translation with Introduction and Commentary*, edited by C. S. Mann. Vol. 26. Garden City. New York: Doubleday & Company. Inc., 1979.

Alcon, Wallace Arthur. "The Great Commission: Disciples. Basic Greek Grammar." *CENQ* 2:4, no. Winter (1959), p. 645.

Babu, Jeevan. *Mission Hermeneutics: Ncci Resource Series*. Nagpur, 1996.

Bruce, Frederick F. "The End of the First Gospel." *The Evangelical Quarterly* 12, (1940), p. 204.

Castleman, Robbie F. "The Last Word: The Great Commission: Ecclesiology." *Themelios* 32, no. 3 (2007), p. 68.

Culver, D. "What Is the Church's Commission? Some Exegetical Issues in Matthew 28:16-20." *Bibliotheca Sacra* CXXV, no. July- September (1968), p. 253.

Dodd, C. H. "The Appearances of the Risen Christ: An Essay in Form Criticism." In *More New Testament Studies*, 12. London, 1968.

Donaldson, T. L. *Jesus on the Mountain: A Study in Matthean Theology* Jsnts. Sheffield: JSOT Press, 1985.

Ellis, I. P. "But Some Doubted." *New Testament Studies* 14, (1967-68), p. 576.

Fanning, Don. "The Great Commission." *JLBTS* 1:2 no. Article 2 (2014), p. 3.

Fee, Gordon D., ed. *Christology and Pneumatology in Romans 8:9-11*. Grand Rapids, MI: William B. Eerdmans Publishing Company, 1996.

Freeman, Hal "The Great Commission and the New Testament: An Exegesis of Matthew 28:16-20." *Southern Baptist Journal of Theology* 1:4, no. Winter (1997), p. 15.

Funk, Robert W. et al. *The Five Gospels: The Search for the Authentic Words of Jesus: New Translation and Commentary*. San Francisco: Harper Collings, 1997.

Grayston. "The Translation of Matthew 28.17." *Journal for the Study of the New Testament* 21, (1984), p. 105.

Green, Joel B. and Max Turner, ed. *Elsewhere: Some Reflections on Paul as a Trinitarian," Jesus of Nazareth: Lord and Christ.* Grand Rapids, MI: William B. Eerdmans Publishing Company, 1994.

Gundry, Robert *Matthew: A Commentary.* Grand Rapids, MI: William B. Eerdmans Publishing Company, 1994.

Hare, D. and D. Harrington. "Make Disciples of All the Nations." *CBQ* 37, (1975), pp. 359-369.

Hiebert, D. Edmond. "An Expository Study of Matthew 28:16-20." *BSAC* 149/595, no. July (1992), p. 352.

Hubbard, B. *The Matthean Redaction of a Primitive Apostolic Commissioning: An Exegesis of Matthew 28:16-20.* Missoula: Scholars Press, 1974.

Kirby, Alan "The Death of Post-Modernism and Beyond." *Philosophy Now: A Magazine of Ideas.*, no. Oct-Nov (2015).

Kwik, R. "Some Doubted." *Expository Times* 77, (1965-66), p. 181.

Lenski, Culver. "Commentary: The Book of Matthew." *JETS* 10/2, no. Spring (1967), p. 555.

Luter Jr., A. Boyd. "Women Disciples and the Great Commission." *Trinity Journal* 16:2, no. Fall (1995), 185.

McKenzie, John L. "The Gospel According to Matthew." In *The Jerome Biblical Commentary II: The New Testament and Topical Articles*, edited by Raymond E. Brown and others, 114. Bangalore: St. Peter's Seminary, 1972.

Meier, J. "Two Disputed Questions in Matt 28:16-20." *Journal of Biblical Literature* 96, no. 3 (1977), pp. 422-424.

Miller, J. "Nations or Gentiles in Matthew 28:19?" *CBQ* 39, (1977), pp. 94-102.

Morris, L. *The Gospel According to Matthew.* Grand Rapids: Eerdmans, 1992.

Moulton, James Hope and et al. *Syntax" Vol. III. A Grammar of New Testament Greek.* Edinburgh: T & T Clark, 1963.

Osborne, Grand R. "Redaction Criticism and the Great Commission: A Case Study toward a Biblical Understanding of Inerrancy" *JETS* 19/2, no. Spring (1976), pp. 76-77.

Patton, Michael, "Representing Christ to a Postmodern World" https://bible.org/article/representing-christ-postmodern-world (accessed on Oct 2015).

Rad, Gerhard von. *Genesis: A Commentary. Otl.* Philadelphia: The Westminster Press, 1973.

Rogers, Cleon. "The Great Commission." *BSAC* 130:519, no. July (1973), pp. 258-259.

Schaberg, J. *The Father, the Son, and the Holy Spirit: The Triadic Phrase in Matthew 28:19b.* Chico, CA: Scholars Press, 1980.

Teeple, H. M. "The Origin of the Son of Man Christology." *JBL*, Sept, (1965).

Thomas, M. M. *Some Theological Dialogue.* Madras: CISRS & CLS, 1977.

Tumma, Anthoniraj *Breaking Barriers: Liberation of Dialogue and Dialogue of Liberation, the Quest of R. Panikkar and Beyond.* Delhi,: ISPCK, 2000.

Wall, Lynne J., "The Great Commission: Biblical Perspective" www.methodist.org.nzp.

Westermann, Claus *Genesis 12-36: A Commentary.* Vol. 2, edited by John J. Scullion. Mimmeapolis: Augsburg Publishing House, 1985.

Williams, R. *Open to Judgement.* London: DLT, 1994.

Zuck, Roy B. "Greek Words for Teach." *Bibliotheca Sacra* CXXI, no. April-June (1965), p. 163.

*Chapter 3*

# SCIENCE, GOOD NEWS AND THE WHOLE CREATION

**P. Dayanandan**[1]

## 1. What is the Good News?

In a Valedictory address[1] at UTC, I urged the out-going students to interpret the present time and tell us what the Good News is all about. The Good News must be repeatedly brought to us because we have either forgotten it or corrupted it. Institutions such as a church or a theological college must struggle to comprehend the message that Jesus conveyed and how it has been interpreted over two thousand years; and how to understand and appreciate the relevance of this message in today's world of challenging philosophies, ideologies, religious faiths and exploding scientific knowledge of the world. The birth, life and teachings of Jesus are undoubtedly a Good News for all. Jesus Himself focused on the Kingdom of God, not on the church, church councils or any other institutions. The imagery he used to explain the kingdom can at first sight be misleading. It is not royal nor heavenly; it is not a treasure nor a pearl. These metaphors imply that the goodness of this kingdom is immeasurable. The Kingdom is here, in the hearts and minds of people, on the earth, as a tiny seed full of life, ready to sprout, as microscopic

1 Dr. Paulraj Dayanandan is a Professor Emeritus and former Head of the Department of Biology at the Madras Christian College, Chennai. This presentation of Dr. Dayanandan during the UTC Alumni Refresher Programme is documented by Mr. Basil Baby Paul and published here after being refined by the presenter.

yeasts ready to multiply and ferment. We are invited to comprehend this and share it with all people, and all creation.

## 2. Comprehending the World

Fulfilling the Great Commission in today's context requires understanding the world we live in today which is vastly different from the world Jesus lived in. Perhaps this is why Jesus wants us to interpret the present time in order to comprehend Him and His message (Lk 12:54-56). Jesus pointed to the rising clouds and blowing wind as phenomena that people were able to correctly interpret during His time. Now, we have just listened for the first time ever to the sound of the gravitational wave that was born 1.3 billion years ago when two black holes merged from a world where gravity was so strong, matter was squeezed into a tiny space from which even light cannot escape. How can we "Go into all the world and preach the gospel to all creation" (Mark 16:15) without a knowledge of all the worlds and all the creations? Knowledge of all kind, not just religious or scientific need to be accessed and interpreted in order present the Good News to this generation. For the Good News was not sealed; it is alive.

It is generally agreed that sacred religious knowledge, including Christian truth and faith, is derived through four major sources that reinforce each other: revelation (enlightenment), tradition, reason and experience.[2] Two other sources of knowledge are, Biblical scholarship and scientific study, both secular in nature with the potential to influence Christian faith. Christian theologians and preacher are not averse to incorporating knowledge generated by Biblical studies. Biblical studies apply rigorous methods of disciplines such as History, Archaeology, Linguistics, Philology, Egyptology and textual criticism for the verification of time and place of Biblical events or authenticating the contents and authorship of the scripture or resolving conflicting accounts of the same events by different authors and the fidelity of the translations from the original. Biblical scholarship can provide new insights and valuable interpretations to re-read the Bible; it can be inspiring but it can also be disturbing when cherished views are sought to be revised. Perhaps the most disturbing of the recent claims is the assertion by some scholars that Jesus and His disciples were not historical persons but allegorical characters created by crypto-Buddhists.[3]

Science is perceived today by some as antithetical to Christian faith thus leading to a variety of responses ranging from denial of scientific worldview to total reliance on a literal reading of the Bible. Others have attempted to use scientific discoveries as support for faith statements. A distinguished evolutionary biologist, Stephen Gould, thought of science and faith as non-overlapping independent magisteria and urged people not to confuse religious discussions in the church with scientific discourse.[4] Ian Barbour categorized the current views of relationship between science and religion into four models: a) as in irreconcilable conflict with each other as one discipline asserts that it alone represents the truth and the other is false; b) as independent domains that can be equally true as long as they do not intrude into each other's claims; c) as in a state of constructive dialogue with each other, respecting the claims of each; d) as science and religion integrating truths acceptable to both in a process that can lead to a more comprehensive worldview and theology.[5] Barbour thought that if the Bible is taken seriously and not literally then the central biblical message could be accepted without accepting non-scientific or pre-scientific biblical cosmology.

Barbour is neither alone nor his typologies new. There has been a long history of reflection on biblical and scientific epistemology of the nature of our world. Commenting on Genesis, before Galileo was born and three hundred years before Darwin, John Calvin said: "To my mind, this is a certain principle, that nothing is here treated of but the visible world. He who would learn astronomy and other recondite arts, let him go elsewhere." Jurgen Moltmann thought that literal biblicists misunderstand the biblical tradition as "laying down once and for all particular findings about nature, and render all further research superfluous". For Moltmann, the creation stories are a part of a hermeneutical process of revision and innovation based on new experiences and insights, and the Bible is not a closed book. Just 300 years after the birth of Christ the great theologian Origen thought that the Bible contained many narratives that did not literally take place, and pleaded for a metaphorical and non-literal reading of Genesis: "What intelligent person can imagine that there was a first day, then a second and third day, evening and morning, without the sun, the moon, and the stars?...Who is foolish enough to believe that, like a human gardener, God planted a garden in Eden in the East and placed in it a tree of life, visible and physical, so that by biting into its fruit one would obtain life? And that by eating from another tree, one would come to know good and evil? And when it is said that God walked in the garden in the evening and that Adam hid himself behind a tree, I cannot imagine that anyone will doubt that these details point symbolically to spiritual meaning by using a historical narrative which did not literally happen."

What science offers is a worldview built and continually being built on a rational method of understanding the world, through logical reasoning, trial and error, falsification of hypotheses, evolving consensus based on evidence, and depending on certain faith that the human mind can comprehend the world. Einstein remarked, "The most incomprehensible thing about the world is that it is comprehensible." This comprehension is not claimed to be an absolute certainty. Charles Darwin, the great unifier of all life, living and extinct and yet to come, wondered about the trustworthiness and ability of the human mind - evolved from lower animals - to comprehend the true nature of reality and existence. This humility in the acceptance of the limitation of our reasoning power indeed reflects a dilemma, but that does not endorse every religious worldview as revealing some absolute truth and replacing scientific enquiry into the nature of the world. A Catholic catechism elegantly explains the relationship between faith and reasoning:

"Though faith is above reason, there can never be any real discrepancy between faith and reason. Since the same God who reveals mysteries and infuses faith has bestowed the light of reason on the human mind, God cannot deny Himself, nor can truth ever contradict truth" (CCC 159).

## 3. Cosmogonies: Creation Myths of Origins

Long before the emergence of the current scientific concepts of Big Bang cosmology and evolutionary theory of life, people throughout the world told stories of how the physical world and animals, plants and humans came about. Hundreds of such creation myths or cosmogonies exist.[6] They satisfied the quest of early people as they sought comforting explanations for their lives amidst a complex interplay of physical and biological forces, benign and cruel. In the Indian subcontinent too, many tribal communities and Vedic and post-Vedic people crafted numerous creation myths. A glaring exception seems to be the Tamil society as we do not find any creation myth in the corpus of the early Tamil literature, the so-called Sangam literature! Creation myths are mega stories, dealing with primal and cosmic themes such as mating, birth, cosmic egg, chaos, sky, cloud, mountain and water. They may also deal with sacrifice, blood and death, underworld, snake, evil and creation out of nothing. The Hebrew Biblical story of creation is one such cosmogony perhaps with its roots going back to the Sumerian myths.[7] The Babylonian story of creation known as "*Enuma Elish" is believed to have been written a few hundred years before the Genesis story was written. The Babylonian story assumes that in the beginning there was chaos and darkness. Light was created first and then successively a firmament, dry land, sun, moon, stars, men and women. After this, God rested and celebrated. This remarkable similarity between the Genesis and Babylonian stories suggest that one must have been derived from the other or both from an earlier common story.*

Creation myths can be elegant and beautiful, with elements of the story seemingly in consonance with some 'scientific' account. Such is the case of the creation myth of the Omaha Indians: all life was once spirits seeking a place to settle; the sun was too hot and the moon too cold; however a mountain emerged out of the sea and eruption of fire dried up the water to create land; life settled on this land first as plants, then animal and then as people.[8] Creation myths can have lasting effects on the cultural, moral and ethical life of societies. Some such as the Rg Vedic origin myth of the humans emerging out of a sacrifice leading to the four *varnas*, have had devastating effects on the society tearing it into unjust hierarchies and suffering. The Biblical accounts of creation too have elements such as 'sin' that when improperly interpreted have the power to frighten people. Again, in spite of the assertion that humans were created in the image of God, we have the story of Noah and his sons to account for the human diversity on earth. Thus, Shem, Ham and Japheth were considered as the ancestors of Semitic and non-Semitic people initiating racist notions and prejudice. Such an explanation had serious consequences for people starting from the conquest of Canaan to slavery and the massacre of South Africans in the Battle of Blood River in Zululand. It was the South African land of the Zulus that the white Boer Voortekkers wanted and even made a covenant with their God as they killed 4,000 black warriors at the Battle of Blood River in 1838.

## 4. Time, History, Cosmology and Evolution

Most Christians are in good company with historians in our academic institutions. Both are comfortable with a restricted period of less than 5,000 years of history of human beings. For pre-historians this is almost the end of the horizon. Any period beyond this is left to the scientific discipline of anthropology. For Christians, Moses may be an historical figure, but Abraham and Noah fade into prehistory. As for Adam and Eve and the creation of the world many enter into a time warp, confusion and arguments. For the Anglican archbishop of Dublin, James Ussher creation occurred in 4004 BC. In 1650, the Anglican archbishop of Dublin, James Ussher published his calculations announcing that the world was created in 4004 BC. The bishop based his calculations on a literal reading of the events and genealogies mentioned in the Bible. We now know that 6000 years before this period there were people already settled and cultivating rye, barley, wheat and fig in Palestine and the Fertile Crescent.

Cosmology and Evolution are two major scientific theories that are engaging the best of scientific minds. Both have great potential to enlighten religious people. In the ultimate analysis both are attempts to update the creation story of our origins and our history. Time and history are important for Christians because we lay considerable emphasis on Jesus as a historical figure and consider this history as an essential part of God's plan and revelation to humans. Conventional history deals with a time period of a few thousand years while Evolution and Cosmology extend this history to about 4 billion years of life on earth, and to about 14 billion years ago when the universe and all ingredients of life and even space and time were born. We will see later that scientists are not concerned with the question of why the universe was born. It is a religious question that science cannot answer.

Scientists reveal that about 14 billion years ago when the 'Big Bang' occurred time and space came into existence. Some have described this moment as the day without a yesterday! More than 1600 years ago the influential Christian theologian and philosopher St. Augustine declared that the "world was made with time, not in time"! Astrophysicists can describe the evolution of the universe from a period as infinitesimally small as $10^{-43}$ second. This was the time when one of the four fundamental forces of nature, namely gravity, separated from the singularity. The subatomic particles that appeared rapidly would later produce atoms and molecules. It took more than ten billion years before life appeared on earth after the Big Bang, and another 3.5 billion years before human beings evolved.

Perhaps the most important aspect of this history is the awesome fact that we humans too are products of this beginning and are governed by the forces, and are made up of particles that were born billions of years ago. Today, these humans have been empowered to detect gravitational waves whose existence was predicted a hundred years ago by Einstein. This is no small achievement, as what was detected was a wave that originated about 1.3 billion years during the collision of two massive black holes and which reached the earth in September 2015 and made it expand and contract about the width of an atomic nucleus. Science will continue to update and even alter the current theories as cosmologists make new discoveries and revise their models; such course corrections are an integral part of scientific enquiry. Yet the larger picture of enormous timescale and space will remain. Any theologizing on creation story should incorporate this emerging scientific understanding of the origin of cosmos.

## 5. Evolution - Creation Debate

Before we explore the current scientific view of evolution of life, including human beings, it might be helpful to place the so called evolution-creation debate in proper perspective.

Some Christian groups have great difficulty accepting either the timescale or the process of origins advanced by science. Although such groups are few in number and based mostly in the USA, they exert strong influence on others, including the youth in India. These 'Biblical literalists' reject the scientific worldview and believe in a universe less than ten thousand years old, in Noachian Flood, and in a six day Special Creation. And some still believe in a Flat Earth too! Those who believe in Special Creation consider the earth to be very young, only 6,000 years old, and that all living things were created in a matter of few days. Some groups in the USA have attempted to block the teaching of evolution in schools and have argued in the courts, unsuccessfully, to introduce Biblical cosmogony as a 'scientific' discipline of 'Creationism' or as 'Intelligent Design' to be taught as an alternate to evolutionary theory in schools.[9] Scientists do not agree that creationism is a science. It is not supported by empirical evidence, and it does not draw its conclusions from observations of nature but on dogmatic belief. Science progresses by making hypotheses that can be tested and accepted or rejected. The assumptions of creationism do not lead to either testable or falsifiable hypotheses.

The unfolding view of the cosmos and its origins have inspired some philosophers and physicists to explore if there is any meaning and purpose for the emergence of intelligent human beings. They point out that several physical constants of the early universe, such as the expansion rate, formation of elements, and particle/antiparticle ratio were all so fine-tuned as to be merely a coincidence. It appears to them that the initial conditions and basic laws of the universe allow for life to evolve; that observers must arise at sometime, even to bring the universe into being; and that intelligent beings would evolve and intelligence would never die out. They have formulated several versions of what is known as the 'Anthropic Principle' such as the Weak and Strong Anthropic Principles to express these concepts.[10] Some take this as evidence that God might have 'designed' such laws for life to originate and evolve and therefore there need be no conflict with the theory of evolution. However, it has been argued that an all-powerful God does not have to depend upon "life-friendly" laws since God's will and power alone are sufficient to create and sustain life. 'Process Thought' philosophers and 'Process Theologians' attempt to incorporate the scientific discoveries. They see nature itself as a dynamic evolutionary process with a long history, and where both chance and law operate to produce complexity in organization of living things and emergence of novelty. There are many scientists and Christians who subscribe to a view known as "Theistic Evolution". They believe that God is an agent of power and intelligence who designed and created the world for a purpose. Some of them agree that God could have created life through a process of evolution and that He might have directly intervened at various points of creation and evolution.

## 6. Current Responses to Scientific Views on Origin of Universe and Evolution

Major non-Christian faiths do not find any difficulty in accepting the scientific views on origin of the universe and evolution of life. In India, this may be partly due to acceptance of a worldview of enormous past timescales, and diversity in divinities and myths. Also, there is no centralized authority, demanding acceptance of a single creed by all people. The Judeo-Christian tradition is not anchored in deep history, yet, except for some Orthodox groups most Jewish people accept scientific theories on origin of universe and evolution. Jewish theologians believe that the Torah reveals God as the creator and addresses the question why God created the world but not how He created it.

A survey of fifty major Christian denominations revealed that only six appeared to use any doctrine of creation.[11] Some groups of fundamentalist Baptist churches and the Assemblies of God have introduced a "Doctrine of Creation" that must be confessed before one becomes a full member of the church. The doctrine requires belief in a 'young-earth' and a literal six-day creation. This 'doctrine' can be traced to the claim of a vision of Seventh Day Adventists who saw the creation of the world in six 24-hour days. Today movements such as Answers in Genesis, the Institute for Creation Research, and Creation Science Evangelism of Kent Hovind promote this doctrine and a literal reading of the Genesis account.

Most Christian denominations do not insist on such strict reading of the Bible and find it possible to accommodate the scientific worldview. For example, all that the ancient Apostolic Creed has to say about creation is "I believe in God, the Father Almighty, the Creator of heaven and earth". And the equally ancient Nicene Creed also demands nothing more than "I believe in one God, the Father

Almighty, maker of heaven and earth, and of all things visible and invisible". The Thirty-Nine articles of faith of the Anglican Church do not demand any belief about creation, and the Creed of Athanasius dating from the fourth century makes no mention of creation. Also, those who formulated statements of faith before Darwin's time (e.g. Westminster Confession) were not aware of the concept of evolution, and some churches are willing to reread the creed just as they are willing to reread the Bible.

Most mainline Protestant denominations do not find scientific views fundamentally opposed to Christian belief. In 2002, the Presbyterian Church (USA) adopted the following resolutions on evolution and education and stated that the church "1. Reaffirms that God is the Creator, in accordance with the witness of Scripture and the Reformed Confessions. 2. Reaffirms that there is no contradiction between an evolutionary theory of human origins and the doctrine of God as Creator. 3. Encourages State Boards of Education across the nation to establish standards for science education in Public Schools based on the most reliable content of scientific knowledge as determined by the scientific community. 4. Calls upon Presbyterian scientists and science educators to assist congregations, presbyteries, communities, and the public to understand what constitutes reliable scientific knowledge."

The Episcopal Church of USA in its Catechism on Creation deals with "Theology of Creation" and "Creation and Science". On creation stories of Genesis chapters 1 and 2 the catechism affirms: "These majestic stories should not be understood as historical and scientific accounts of origins but as proclamations of basic theological truths about creation. Creation in Holy Scripture refers to and describes the relationship between God and all God's wonderful works." Genesis 2 is understood to be "in poetic and metaphorical language", emphasizing "God's immanence or intimate relationship with creation." "The Bible, including Genesis, is not a divinely dictated scientific textbook. We discover scientific knowledge about God's universe in nature not Scripture." The Catechism has bold questions on creation and accepts the major scientific views on "Big Bang" cosmology, the long timescales of billions of years, and biological evolution. In 2006, Dr. Rowan Williams, the Archbishop of Canterbury and leader of the Church of England, cautioned against teaching of creationism since it could reduce the true meaning of the Biblical doctrine of creation. He asserted that the Biblical stories did not belong in the same category as evolutionary theory.

The Evangelical Lutheran Church in America 'has not enforced an official position on creation or evolution allowing members to embrace positions ranging from strict creationism to Theistic evolution.' The Lutheran Church (Missouri Synod) on the other hand prefers a more literal reading of the creation story in the Bible. The United Methodist Church in USA also does not have an official statement on any theories of evolution. However, that Church recognizes that scientific account of "cosmological, geological and biological evolution are not in conflict with theology." The Eastern Orthodox Church has liberal views on creation. It does not find any serious conflict with the scientific worldview. Although, it accepts Adam and Eve formally as first human beings it does not take the Genesis text literally.

The Roman Catholic Church has made periodic statements that make its stand clear on cosmology and evolution. The Pontifical Academy of Sciences, a scientific body of the Vatican, established in 1936 by Pope Pius XI, provides authoritative inputs on scientific developments to the church. With regard to cosmology the Catholic Church affirms God created the universe out of nothing but it has no official position on the process of creation, whether all at once or over immense time periods. In 1950, Pope Pius XII made statements on biological evolution that have permitted the teaching of evolution in schools. In his letter (encyclical, Humani Generis) to all Roman Catholic Bishops in the world the Pope observed that Church does not forbid research and discussions on the doctrine of evolution and that the theory of evolution was a "serious hypothesis, worthy of further research and reflection (along with research and reflection on opposing theories)." It did not forbid inquiry into the origin of the human body as coming from pre-existent and living matter. However, it believed that even if the body developed from previous life forms, still God directly created soul. Pope John Paul II confirmed these views in his 1986 General Audience: "the theory of natural selection, understood in a sense that does not exclude divine causality, is not in principle opposed to the truth about the creation of the visible world as presented in the Book of Genesis...this hypothesis proposes only a probability, not a scientific certainty. The doctrine of faith, however, invariably affirms that man's spiritual soul is directly created by God...it is possible that the human body, following the order impressed by the Creator on the energies of life, could have been gradually prepared in the forms of antecedent living beings."

In 1996, Pope John Paul II (Message to Pontifical Academy of Science, 1996) added that "new findings lead us toward the recognition of evolution as more than a hypothesis", and that "Even if the human body originates from pre-existent living matter, the spiritual soul is spontaneously created by God." Pope Benedict XVI reaffirmed the Catholic position in his address in 2006 to the Congregation for the Doctrine of the Faith in the Vatican saying that "The Church joyfully accepts the real conquests of human knowledge" and that science should help the faithful understand "the mysteries of life on Earth" and see "the logic of faith in God." A statement released by the Pontifical Academy of Sciences in 2008 further clarifies the latest stand of the Catholic Church: "The extraordinary progress in our understanding of evolution and the place of man in nature should be shared with everyone. . . . Furthermore, scientists have a clear responsibility to contribute to the quality of education, especially as regards the subject of evolution." In 2014, Pope Francis addressed the Pontifical Academy of Sciences declaring that the theories of evolution and the Big Bang are real and God is not "a magician with a magic wand." As far as the Catholic Church is concerned this effectively puts an end to the "pseudo theories" of creationism and intelligent design.

## 7. The Evolutionary View of Life

During the past 150 years since Charles Darwin published his views on the evolution of species - he called it descent with modification - all disciplines of science have offered overwhelming support to his theory. In his influential book, The Phenomenon of Man, published in 1955 the Jesuit priest and theologian Pierre Teilhard de Chardin described evolution as a process that lead to increasing complexity and observed, "Evolution is a light which illuminates all facts, a curve that all lines must follow." Following this the renowned geneticist and evolutionary biologist and a Russian Orthodox Christian, Theodosius Dobzhansky, wrote an essay in 1973 with a title that is still widely used to emphasize the central role of evolution in biology: "**Nothing in biology makes sense except in the light of evolution**." Dobzhansky also observed: "It is a blunder to mistake the Holy Scriptures for elementary textbooks of astronomy, geology, biology, and anthropology. Only if symbols are construed to mean what they are not intended to mean can there arise imaginary, insoluble conflicts.... the blunder leads to blasphemy: the Creator is accused of systematic deceitfulness" and "It is ludicrous to mistake the Bible and the Koran for primers of natural science. They treat of matters even more important: the meaning of man and his relations to God."

A number of organic chemicals have been synthesized from inorganic material under conditions that simulate Earth's primitive atmosphere and energy sources, and the origin of life continues to be an intense field of research. Although we have no knowledge of the existence of life outside Planet Earth, the recent discovery of more than 2,000 'Exoplanets' that orbit other solar systems have revived the interest in searching for life outside our solar system The new discipline of astrobiology is devoted to questions of the origin and evolution of life here on earth and elsewhere, as well as to its future.

Darwin's greatest contribution is the unification of all life as related members of a large family, often depicted as a tree of life.[12] The chimpanzee is the closest living species related to humans with about 98% similarity in DNA. In the past there had been other close relatives, now extinct, but some of their fossil remains are yielding DNA that can be analyzed and compared with our own. If chimpanzee is our distant cousin so are the neem tree and the bacteria. What distinguishes humans from all other life is the acquisition and use of symbolic language, the presence of cultural evolution alongside biological evolution, and a post-human future where humans have the ability to modify their own environment and future. The advancement in DNA technology has now reached a point where it may even be possible to bring back extinct species from their DNA remains.

Evolution is also history. It is a history where the landmarks appear in millions of years. What evolution reveals is that all living things, including human beings, are descendants of common ancestors, and that all life – including the estimated 30 million living and nearly 600 million extinct species - are truly and organically related to each other. **Biodiversity is a product of evolution**. Evolution links all life to matter, to the elementary particles, energy and the four fundamental forces, laws of physics and the very beginning of space and time. These are awesome facts that can no longer be ignored from any theologizing on life and the human condition.

## 8. Origin of Humans and Migration Out of Africa

As with all living organisms, human beings are descendants of preexisting ancestral species. Our immediate ancestry has been traced back to a few species of now extinct African hominins. There is general agreement that we, *Homo sapiens*, emerged as a species, in Africa, about 200,000 years ago. The science of genetics is now so advanced that by studying the mutations in DNA it is possible to determine the relationships between human groups and trace the time and route of migration of our ancestors across the globe. It is even possible to determine the extent of interbreeding that might have occurred with other extinct human species as our ancestors traveled the globe. Powerful techniques of DNA analysis have revealed that all human beings, 7 billion living and an estimated 140 billion dead, are descendants of one woman who lived about 180,000 years ago, somewhere in East Africa. This "ancestral mother" has been nicknamed "African Eve" and "Mitochondrial Eve." There were other women in this small group of our early ancestors; however for some reason, only the progenies of this one woman survived to populate Africa and the world. The Y-chromosomes of all men can also be traced to one man, an "African Adam."

How do we account for the incredible physical and cultural diversity of people all over the globe and in India? About one hundred thousand years ago there were no human beings anywhere else on the Earth except in the African Continent. About 70,000 years ago there began one of the most dramatic episodes of human migration, of a small group of people who ventured out of Africa to colonize the rest of the continents. In this African group were the ancestors of all people of the world - Blacks, Whites, Jews, Arabs, Dalits, Adivasis, Japanese and Mexican, and everyone else. We are all Africans in our ancestry, and Africa is the home of our forefathers and foremothers. Recent studies reveal that as people migrated out of Africa they interbred with a now extinct human species, the Neanderthals. All people outside of Africa carry 1-4% Neanderthal DNA and my genetic makeup includes 1% Neanderthal DNA! The National Genographic Project alone has tested the DNA of more than 740,000 people from more than 140 countries to determine the pattern of migration of their maternal and paternal ancestors.[13]

India was one of the earliest settled places outside Africa, settled some 60,000 years ago by a group traveling along a coastal route. It was from the Indian subcontinent that some groups migrated further to Southeast Asia and Australia.

There was another wave of migration about 30,000 years that resulted in large-scale settlement of the inland. Besides these two waves of migration there have been many other episodes of migration until modern times, resulting in the enormous genetic diversity of the South Asian population, a diversity next only to the great African genetic diversity. Indian scientists and their international collaborators are now revealing how various groups intermixed to produce a completely hybridized Indian population. It was this diversity that has been divided, compartmentalized and arranged in hierarchies resulting in about 4,700 major communities and more than 50,000 endogamous sub-castes or *jati* groups.

A small sample of DNA, say from blood cells, a buccal swab, a root hair or even from a 30,000 years old fossil bone fragment is all that is needed for modern scientists to trace the migratory history of our maternal or paternal ancestors. The DNA in mitochondria and the DNA in the Y-chromosome can be analyzed to infer history of migration of maternal and paternal ancestors. I have tested my DNA for the history of my ancestors. I share a common ancestral mother with more than 50% of other Indians. About 50,000 years ago, while migrating out of Africa or while in the Arabian Peninsula this woman had a mutation in her mitochondrial DNA. That mutation has been inherited by all her descendants. I can trace my paternal ancestry to a man who lived about a thousand generations ago. His descendants carry a mutation in their Y-chromosome that identify them as members of a branch known as "H1-Haplogroup". This same man is also the ancestor of many groups in other parts of the world and India. My paternal ancestor is also the ancestor of men in 30 different castes and tribes of Tamil Nadu.

We Indians all have a highly mixed heritage. Tribal, caste and other divisions have very little meaning at the genetic level and there exists no caste, *gotra* or *jati* that is genetically 'pure.' Caste is not biologically determined; it was created by a racist, prejudicial and exploitative ideology that divided people and justified the division by constructing false concepts of biological determinants. This may be a scientific fact; but this is precisely how Jesus envisaged the human family, as all people being His sisters and brothers. Can we reword Acts 17:26 and ask Luke to say: 'From **one African Eve** and **one Y-Chromosomal Adam** he created every nation of humankind to live on all the face of the earth'?

## 9. Is Science a Challenge to Faith?

Not if we listen to Jesus who says: You know how to interpret the appearance of earth and sky but why do you not know how to interpret the present time? (Lk 12:54-56). In the past two thousand years science has changed our understanding of the sky, earth and the world and all that dwell in it. We are not forbidden now to interpret the meaning of all this new knowledge and relate it to the ever present quest for Kingdom values. Jesus used riddles (parables) and aphorisms to appeal to our minds and we are not forbidden to use logic, reasoning and common sense to make sense of the world.

Yes, science will be a challenge to faith if we choose to be biblical literalists and alienate all inquiring minds. Whatever we may chose, science is here to stay, not in order to counter any religious beliefs but to continue to ask questions about the world and also benefit from the technologies it generates. Ninety percent of the scientists that ever lived are now engaged in the pursuit of extraordinary developments in many fields.[14] Computer science, biotechnology, artificial intelligence, nanotechnology and quantum physics have emerged as major fields. Within the next fifty years we are likely to see scientific achievements that surpass the achievements of the past four hundred years. We live in a 'century of biology' and new discoveries in biological science are predicted to dramatically alter health, economy and ethics of people. DNA technologies offer for the first time in scientific endeavor the ability to bring back to life extinct life forms. This new field of "De-extinction" has already achieved some small success with preserved cells of an extinct frog, in an experiment labeled the 'Lazarus Project.'[15] Scientists are now targeting some twenty four other extinct animals for de-extinction projects.

Science and religion as distinct fields of enquiry may also change as science attempts to answer several questions of human behavior and spiritual experience. Sociobiologists such as E. O. Wilson claim that science can replace theology as an explanatory discipline of religious experience. The modern discipline of 'evolutionary psychology' that has replaced sociobiology is now attempting to show that moral behavior too can ultimately be explained as an outcome of biological processes and gene expression. Evolutionary biologists believe that such cherished values as love, altruism, compassion, empathy, shame, humility, moral outrage, honor, self-respect and remorse may all have a purely genetic and biochemical basis. These assertions, when substantiated, will pose new challenges in interpreting the commandments of Jesus regarding how we should relate to our neighbors. An emerging field of theology known as 'neurotheology' or 'biotheology' attempts to provide a neurological explanation for certain religious, spiritual and mystical experiences.[16] Correlation between brain activity and subjective states of spiritual experience has led to the possibility of experimental induction of such 'spiritual' states through stimulation of brains centers. William James published his much-acclaimed book *The Varieties of Religious Experience* more than a hundred years ago, in 1902. Neurotheology may show that many of these religious experiences have an evolutionary and biochemical basis. We are reminded of what John Calvin wrote in his influential 1559 book, *Institutes of the Christian Religion*: "There is within the human mind, and indeed by natural instinct, an awareness of divinity."

How do youth respond to these developments in science? How are they likely to respond to unexpected and astonishing developments likely to emerge within decades? The Barna Group, a Christian polling firm in the USA, released results in 2011 that showed many young people leaving the church because they see it as antagonistic to science.[17] Other reasons for feeling disconnected with the church include: Christians are too confident they know all the answers (35%); Churches are out of step with the scientific world we live in (29%); Christianity is anti-science (25%); and turned off by the creation versus evolution debate (23%). This can happen to youth anywhere in the world, including India. Indian Non-Christians are free to use science as an epistemology for understanding the world without fear of any institution castigating them. Light of knowledge cannot and should not be kept hidden under a basket. It is unfortunate that our major Protestant churches and theological institutions have no statements to make on major issues such as cosmology and evolution, and also do not include a sufficient space for appropriate science curriculum in theology programs.

## 10. Can Science Answer all Questions?

Science is not the only source of knowledge nor a perfect solution to the problems of the world. There are thousands of scientists who maintain high ethical standards in their research, communication and application of their findings. Science and technology are also used by some scientists and many corporations to exploit people and make unfair profits, and by governments to dominate the world with military and economic power and perpetuate newer forms of colonialism. Yet the minds that asked questions about their world and generated a thousand cosmogonies in the past will continue to ask new questions and expect answers for them. What is surprising is that all questions we ask cannot be answered by science! We need theologians and philosophers and storytellers! Just as we do not look into Scriptures for determining the nature of the force that help two bodies attract each other, nor explore if DNA is present on the moon or mars so also we do not look into our astronomy textbooks to find out why the universe exists or into our biology textbooks to understand the meaning of life.

The questions that science attempts to answer are mostly the 'how' questions, and not 'why' questions. Thus, science can ask and attempt to answer 'how' the universe began and evolve but it cannot answer the question 'why' the universe came into existence. Science can attempt to answer how life originated and evolved but it cannot deal with the question of why life exists on earth. Such 'why' questions are religious or philosophical questions. The table below lists several topics for which the why and how questions are more profitably addressed either by religion or by science. There are also questions that are in the exclusive religious domain. Science, for example, cannot deal with either the why or how of the goal of history, and meaning of life and death. We must also agree that the answers provided by religion for the why questions need not satisfy everyone.

| The big issues | Science mostly deals with 'how' questions | Theology mostly deals with 'why' and 'what' questions |
|---|---|---|
| Universe | How did the universe evolve? | Why does the universe exist? |
| Universe | How will the universe evolve? | Why should there be a future? |
| Life | How did life originate? | Why should there be life? |
| Human beings | How did humans evolve? | Why are there humans? |
| Human Behavior | What controls human behavior? | Why are people what they are? |
| Suffering | How we feel physical pain? | Why there is suffering? |
| Goal of history | - | What is the goal of history? |
| Meaning of life/death | - | What is the meaning of life? |
| Truth/Goodness/ Beauty | - | Why do they exist? |
| Evil | - | What is it & Why it exists? |
| Faith, Hope, Love | - | Why we need hope, faith, etc.? |

## 11. Science, Suffering and Theodicy

Catastrophic physical phenomena such as tsunami, hurricane and earthquake can cause immense damage and pain to people. How does one respond to these? Science offers intelligible explanations for these physical phenomena and sound biological explanations for the phenomenon of pain. For Christians, understanding suffering in a world governed by a God who is good, loving, caring and comforting is indeed a theological problem - a problem described as 'theodicy'. Quite often sinfulness is evoked as the reason for the occurrence of devastating events. This is what happened during the tsunami of December 2004 that killed 250,000 people. The response of many conservative Christians around the world to the tsunami was that God sent it to punish and warn people against evil, hatred, and moral turpitude. Thus, it was a vengeful act against human rebellion. They saw a connection between the tsunami and a variety of activities - fornication and sexual perversion, increase in rate of abortion, and the number of gay and lesbian people. They asserted that there is no such thing as 'innocent' suffering since all are sinners and that babies too are sinners by nature. Others believed that the tsunami was sent for a greater good of God bringing people to God. Yet others see a clear sign of the last days of thė end of the world.

When asked to talk on the title "Did God send the Tsunami?" I found it difficult to address this question in a manner that could satisfy all listeners.[18] However, it was not all that difficult to provide an answer that satisfied most and made everyone to reflect when the question was turned around: "Did the Son of God send the Tsunami?" Such a reversal leads to several questions such as: Would one who promised to offer life abundant cause death? How can one who ignored the stirring of the pool and healed the man by the poolside send a sea storm? Can he who calmed the sea and walked on placid waters rejoice in sending killer waves? How can one who healed and gave sight to people send disease and afflictions? Would he who multiplied the fish, bread and wine cause famine and thirst? Would he who loved the children and hugged them make orphans out of them? How can he impose burden, after calling the heavy-laden to come to him for rest? Did he not want people to go free and not get caught in bondage? Can a shepherd who shows the way be a source of confusion? How can one who told Satan to shut up, allow him to unleash the demonic force of a Tsunami? Did the Son of God who said that He came to save, not to judge and who was a loving friend of the sinners and adulterers send the Tsunami to punish people?

The inevitable conclusion is that God is not responsible for such calamities or the suffering that follows. This may only be a partial answer to the problem of theodicy since the suffering is real and unmitigated by any thought of absolving God from not being in control of such disasters. It does not mean that praying for fair weather, and praying again to thank for enjoying such weather are illogical. We pray not to ask for God to physically interfere with the direction of a moving cloud or blow the wind in some other direction. Rather we pray to focus on goodness that prevails that is beyond human creative powers, survival in the midst of disaster, and hope, assurance and possibilities of better times.

## 12. Science, Great Commission and the Whole Creation

We can ask again how to "Go into all the world and preach the gospel to all creation" (Mark 16:15) without a knowledge of all the worlds and all the creations? In the original Greek, all of creation meant the cosmos. Whatever other translation we may use - 'whole creation', 'everyone', 'all people', 'every creature' - the Great Commission cannot be confined to the human species. The whole creation as we know it today consists of a universe full of galaxies, perhaps many such universes and matter, energy and phenomena of truly cosmic scale. Life as we know it is a manifestation in one such galaxy, the Milky Way galaxy, in a tiny solar system. Science reveals previously unimagined views of beauty and complexity in the cosmos as well as in ecosystems and inside the cells and atoms. Science provides us greater appreciation of the grandeur of creation. It helps us update the story of our place and history in the cosmos. For those who are contemplating on the power of the Creator, science deepens their sense of mystery of time and space, and relatedness of all things in the universe. Science does not detract but adds to the proper interpretation of the Logos -- structure of cosmos, Good News of Jesus -- and can help avoid superstitious and fanatical dogmas.

Science helps us reexamine traditional Christian views on role and place of humans in creation and human responsibility as we find the creation groaning and in bondage. A recent example of productive dialogue between science and religion is the development of theologies and action programs to respond to the environmental crisis. Science revealed the intensity of the environmental crisis affecting land, water, air and biodiversity, and the role of the human species in the ongoing sixth major extinction. Theologians responded by re-reading the Bible and reinterpreting the Genesis account and developed such disciplines as ecotheology, theology of land, land ethics, feminist ecotheology, process theology, animal theology and green theology towards maintaining the integrity of creation. People responding to such theologies tend to care for the environment and also sympathize with the attempts of scientists to protect and conserve nature and new creation. This can never be a holistic response without the knowledge that biodiversity is a product of evolution and that all life is organically related through evolutionary history.

Science is optimistic in approach – more food can be produced, newer sources of energy can be developed, species can be conserved, diseases can be eradicated, and the mysteries of universe revealed. While all may not agree that science can bring unconditional good, the tone of optimism inherent in science can counter and balance the pessimistic aspects of religion such as threat of punishment for sin and imminent apocalyptic end of the world. For those who believe that truth can set one free, scientific truths are certainly worth pursuing. Both science and religion promise a new world. The success and failure of science, and the doubts and conflicts of scientists all can provide raw material for theologians. Religion in turn can have a moderating effect on science that has potential to create technologies that can unleash destructive power, physical, moral and psychological. The cold objective and rational approach of science cannot warm the hearts and minds of people longing for justice, peace, joy, love and meaning in life. Neither can a literal reading of the Bible or the scriptures of other faiths ever satisfy the same mind. Literal reading can only postpone the possibility of growing, understanding and visioning. Paul Davies, a quantum physicist specializing in cosmology and astrobiology, finds a larger role for science as he states: "It may seem bizarre, but in my opinion science offers a surer path to God than religion … science has actually advanced to the point where what were formerly religious questions can be seriously tackled."[19]

Jesus' Great Commission included the commandment to teach everything he had taught (Mathew 28:20). How does one teach without knowledge and tools and interpreting the present time? Good News always accompanied contemporary knowledge, wisdom, worldview and technology. Jesus taught through aphorisms and parables. Missionaries brought the Good News along with their contemporary knowledge of science, medicine and technology such as printing press and crafts, even a magic lantern to project images. Now knowledge about ourselves and the world has grown many thousand fold. This knowledge includes scientific and biblical scholarship. Christians should access this knowledge. The scientific assertion that all people are descendants of an African Eve is in remarkable consonance with the Christian foundational belief that all people are brothers and sisters and children of one God. Good News to all creation can also be interpreted to reflect the fundamental evolutionary principle that all species that ever lived and are now living are genetically related.

## 13. Church and the Whole Creation

The whole creation cannot be fitted into a church however big we may build it. The whole creation is out in the Kingdom of God, waiting to be renewed as the new creation. Our context for carrying out the Great Commission should be both the world of knowledge and also the church. Pitting science against faith can distract from more serious challenges within religious institutions. Rather than asking if science is a challenge to faith we may want to ask if issues of power, justice, money, greed, prejudice and casteism are a challenge to faith. All these are present in our churches and therefore even church and its structures are also a challenge to faith. The Great Commission is to bring the Good News of a new earth, of new values to all creation. Talking in tongues, proclaiming apocalyptic eschatology, celebrating endless festivals and rituals, revival and healing meetings, in-group gatherings, prosperity gospels, preoccupation with elections, positions of power, nepotism, control of money, corruption and pursuit of distorted theologies and manufactured episcopacy are not uncommon in our churches. These pose greater challenges to the Great Commission and spread of the Good News. They progressively shrink the space of the Kingdom into hundreds of fragmented walled camps of selfish and insecure people. Waving the hand to make the audience fall down is not a miracle. After all no one has turned water into wine in the past two thousand years; and no one will in the future. Doing miracles today is participating in justice and liberation movements, shedding wealth and riches and sharing fish and bread with all people.

The Good News first reached the Indian shores more than 1,500 years ago. Since then several other agents have brought the Good News to us in obedience to the Great Commission. How authentic was this Good News?[20] Have we continued to listen to the authentic Good News? All societies are saddled with ills that constrain the spread of the Good News. India, however, is the most difficult soil for the seed to germinate - caste in Christianity is more powerful than birds, thorns or a rocky soil. Caste choked the seedlings and continues to choke them even today. As long as groups practice caste distinctions they could not be and have never been agents of the Great Commission. To this extent, we must accept that the seed has indeed fallen on a bad soil and the yeast has not been fermenting in India. Without annihilating caste in Christianity India can never deliver the Good News to the whole creation. It is never too late to prepare the soil and let the seed sprout and the tree flourish.[21]

Recent surveys have characterized Indians as: selfish and greedy, less compassionate, less sensitive, more intolerant, violent and xenophobic and divided on the basis of race, class, caste, gender, religion, urban, rural, advanced and backward. Caste continues wield its power of discrimination among people of all religions, including Christians.[22] Christians should understand that they are very much a part of this society and indeed suffer from the evils that are against the values of the Kingdom that Jesus envisaged. They need help to reorient themselves and learn to deal with the human dilemma before the Good News of Jesus can be taken to all people, other life and even non-life, the whole creation. That requires a willingness to work in the new earth, for Kingdom values, outside the constraints of the church and institutions. We need an updated Jesus and His updated Gospel.[23] The Good News must be available for all people, not just a chosen few, and it should be interpreted to be in resonance with our times as if Jesus was born just 30 years ago, and preaching to a crowd on the beach today.

While the truth and central message of the gospel remains the same we now have new knowledge and new tools, and new parables and aphorisms appropriate for this age. The new earth needs new knowledge, all knowledge. Jesus might ask: can you interpret my message with all the knowledge now at your disposal? Who do you think I am? What does my Kingdom mean to you? Do you think I have any Good News for animals? Are plants and fields your neighbors? If you have not learned to love your fellow humans when will you learn to love my non-human sisters and brothers? Why do I continue to seek justice and freedom? Have you re-examined my Nazareth manifesto in light of the current realities in your country? What do you think I meant by end-times? Can you preach the gospel to all creation? Jesus might gently pat you and say: **"Go ahead and access all knowledge, even scientific knowledge, surely I would be with you always, even to the end of the age."**

## References

1. Dayanandan, P. The Master's Thesis. Valedictory Address, The United Theological College, Bangalore, 25th March 2001. Published in: Bangalore Theological Forum, June 2001, 218-224.
2. Catherine Baker and J. B. Miller (eds). *The Evolution Dialogues: Science, Christianity, and the Quest for Understanding*. AAAS, NY, 2007.
3. Lockwood, M. *Buddhism's Relation to Christianity: A Miscellaneous Anthology with Occasional Comment*. T. R. Publications, Chennai, 2014.
4. Gould, S. J. *The Book of Life*. W. W. Norton & Company, NY, 2001.

5. Barbour, I. G. *When Science Meets Religion.* Harper Collins, NY, 2000.
6. Hamilton, V. *In the Beginning: Creation Stories from Around the World.* Houghton Mifflin Harcourt, Boston, 1991.
7. Clifford, R. J. *The Hebrew Scriptures and the Theology of Creation.* Theological Studies, 46.3, (Sep. 1, 1985), 507.
8. Creation stories. http://www.mythencyclopedia.com/Ca-Cr/Creation-Stories.html.
9. Baker C. and Miller, J. B. *The Evolution Dialogues: Science, Christianity, and the Quest for Understanding.* AAAS, Washington, 2007. Cootsona, G. S. *Creation and Last Things: At the Intersection of Theology and Science.* Geneva Press, Louisville, 2002.
10. Bostrom, N. *Anthropic Bias: Observation Selection Effects in Science and Philosophy.* Routledge, NY, 2002. Gribbin, J. and M. Rees. *Cosmic Coincidence: Dark Matter, Mankind, and Anthropic Cosmology.* Bantam Books, NY, 1989.
11. Religious Groups' Views on Evolution. (2014). Pew Research Center http://www.pewforum.org/2009/02/04/religious-groups-views-on-evolution/
12. Dayanandan, P. The Descent of Humans and the Darwinian unification of all life, in *Nature at Work - Ongoing saga of evolution.* V. P. Sharma (ed). National Academy of Sciences: Springer (India), 2010.
13. The Human Story. The National Geographic's Genographic Project. https://genographic.nationalgeographic.com/
14. Kaku, Michio. *Physics of the Future: How Science Will Shape Human Destiny and Our Daily Lives by the Year 2100.* Anchor Press, NY, 2012.
15. The Lazarus Project: Scientists' quest for de-extinction. http://www.smh.com.au/technology/sci-tech/the-lazarus-project-scientists-quest-for- deextinction-20150417-1mng6g.html
16. Newberg, A. B. *Principles of Neurotheology.* Routledge, UK, 2010.
17. You Lost Me: Why Young Christians are Leaving Church. Barna Group study, in *You Lost Me.* Barna, Ventura, CA, 2011.
18. Dayanandan, P. Did God Send the Tsunami? Christian Reflections on Science and Religion. SCM seminar on "Students for Science and Spirituality", 2005. Asia Pacific YMCA Sept 2005, Vol. 30, No.1, p. 4-7. http://www.asiapacificymca.org/publication/magazine/Final-AY-Sept%2005.pdf
19. Paul Davies, *God and the New Physics*, Penguin, 1983, p. 9.
20. Dayanandan, P. The Authentic Good News: Listening from the Shore. *Arasaradi Journal of Theological Reflecton 20*: 1-13, 2007.
21. Dayanandan, P. Annihilation of Caste in Christianity? https://www.academia.edu/s/f9f6636c96
22. Survey on caste practices in India, 2014. http://www.ncaer.org/news_details.php?nID=89
23. Dayanandan, P. We Need an Updated Jesus and His Gospel, NCCI Review Vol. 130: 46-55, 2010.

*Chapter 4*

# "JOINING IN WITH THE SPIRIT OF GOD AT THE PUBLIC SPHERE"
## A PUBLIC THEOLOGY OF MISSION FOR TODAY

**Gnana Patrick**[1]

### 1. Journeying with Mission

The great mission command of Jesus, as presented by the evangelists, is to "proclaim the good news to the whole creation" (Mk. 16: 15) and "make disciples of all nations" (Mt. 28:19) by announcing "repentance and forgiveness of sins" (Lk. 24:47). It was an invitation to believe in the arrival of the Reigning of God with its ultimate freedom for the whole of creation. It was a call which emerged, not just at the end of Jesus' mission, but through the life, death, and resurrection of Jesus, and was given out unto the eschatological times, and that took root in history as an event of mission.

Early Christians gave meaning to this mission through a life of sharing and sacrifice. By witnessing to their faith in Jesus even through excruciating death, they gave unfathomable depth to the event of mission. Paul, with his reflection and missionary activities, constructed a theological horizon to this event of mission. Good News, in his theological vision, stood for redemption from human

1 Prof. Gnana Patrick is the Chairperson of the Department of Christian Studies, University of Madras, Chennai.

sinfulness through the justifying faith (Rom. 1:17), resulting in the 'freedom of the children of God' (Rom. 8: 21; Gal. 5:1).

Patristic era added its own semantic layer to the mission command. The Church became the definitive embodiment of mission. Augustine of Hippo portrayed the Church analogous to Noah's ark to take humanity on board from the deluge of sinfulness that continuously engulfed them. Doctrines developed through a critical process of approval and disapproval, after which the Church, along with its structures and creed, became the visible reality to be created everywhere by Christian mission. The long period until the birth of the Reformation had lived with this ecclesio-centric vision of mission.

The Reformation era shifted the site of mission from the Church to the believer, the human person. Experiencing directly the divine revelation through the help of the scriptures, the believer had to decide for or against God, in order to avail the eternal life destined for the children of God. Bondage of the will, suffered due to the depravity of human nature, had to be overcome with the aid of Divine Grace, approached through faith alone. Consequent upon this realisation, the event of mission came to centre round the act of proclamation, the evangelical act mediating the promise of salvation to the believer. Reading, understanding and preaching the word of God became a desideratum for the event of mission during the Reformation era.

It may be said that our global world shifts the site of our mission to the wider public. Public is the space where different others, even incommensurably different others meet, converse, and have their living and being. This is a space that is constituted by plurality of religions, ethical doctrines, cultural traditions, scientific disciplines, and ideologies besides social, cultural, economic and political activities and systems. In this space, the Church and the believer are certainly the visible agents of mission, but they do it inter-subjectively, listening to the voices heard from the different others.

Let me very briefly introduce here the context and concern of public theology:

Public theology is born in the context of the emergence of public religion. Jose Casanova, in his *Public Religion in the Modern World*, [2] published in 1994, spoke of the emergence of *public religion* in the western context. He thought of it as a reality implicated or involved in the processes of the public sphere, consequent upon what he called the 'de-privatization' of religion. His thesis found support from those who had begun to re-think the theory of secularisation and to

2 Cf. Jose Casanova, *Public Religion in the Modern World* (Chicago: Chicago University Press, 1994).

speak about 'de-secularization', [3] 'return of the religious', [4] 'post-secularity', etc.[5] Furthering his idea, Casanova, in a relatively recent article, has argued that the reality of public religion is found all over the world today.

Religion has gone or goes public in the Indian context too. Indian civil sphere is being enriched with increasingly growing religious initiatives, even while being faced with acute problems on account of religion. The democratic political system - with its activities of mobilisation, electioneering, and representative politics - is increasingly taking to religion in a conspicuous manner. The state mechanism, in its parliament, judiciary, and bureaucracy, is grappling with religious issues more frequently. The very democratic polity has come to be challenged on its 'secular' credentials due to the emergence of 'public religion'.

Public theologies[6] are the 'creative wings' of public religion, with a force of value-oriented conviction based on transcendental frames for commitment in the public sphere. They come with the possibility for transforming the public into a site of peace and harmony, nurtured with values of freedom, justice, equality, dignity, fulfilment of basic necessities, and healthy identity negotiations! It is this promise which inspires us to explore the potentials of public theologies today.

They seek to build upon the existing political, liberation and contextual theologies. While these theologies are also public in an important sense, the 'wider public', the public where *multiple others* are present remains still an external reality to the pursuit of political theologies. For example, a Dalit theology in the Indian context motivates the Christian public to interrogate the inhuman hierarchy of caste; but it does not embark, as a conscious theological endeavour,

---

3 Cf. Peter L. Berger, ed. *The Desecularization of the World: Resurgent Religion and World Politics* (Washington, DC: Ethics and Public Policy Centre, 1999).

4 Cf. Gianni Vattimo, "The Trace of the Trace," in *Religion,* ed. Jacques Derrida and Gianni Vattimo, trans. David Webb *et. al.*(Stanford: Stanford University Press, 1998); Gianni Vattimo and Rene Girard, eds. *Christianity, Truth, and Weakening of Faith – A Dialogue* (New York: Columbia University Press, 2006).

5 Charles Taylor characterises the present 'secular' age as one open as much to religion as to the modern reason – Cf. Charles Taylor, *A Secular Age* (Cambridge: Belknap Press of Harvard University Press, 2007); Jurgen Habermas has come to open himself up to the possibility of religion playing a positive role in the public sphere (when translated into intelligible language) for the moral regeneration of humanity - Cf. Jurgen Habermas and Joseph Ratzinger, *Dialectics of Secularization – On Reason and Religion* (San Francisco: Ignatius Press, 2006); Thus, we see an array of viewpoints upon the resurgence of religion in our secular / post-secular era, and its role in the public sphere.

6 I consciously address them in plural, as John de Gruchy does in the South African context, because they can only be so in the multiple configurations of public spheres to which they respond or in which they are involved. Cf. John W. De. Gruchy, "From Political to Public Theologies: The Role of Theology in Public Life in South Africa," in *Public Theology for the 21st Century – Essays in Honour of Duncan Forrester,* ed. William F. Storrar and Andrew Morton 45-64. London: T & T Clark, 2004. However, when it refers to the generic notion, it is rendered in singular.

upon the responsibility of motivating the wider public, constituted by religious and non-religious others, to interrogate the reality of caste. Public theology, on the other hand, takes up the challenge of interrogating the public realities through a theological vision – a vision constituted in solidarity with religious and 'secular' others. It envisions a characteristically different public engagement wherein the whole public becomes a theological category. In its constitution, the 'incommensurably different comprehensive doctrines'[7] (religions, ethical doctrines, humanist ideologies, etc) are brought together in an interactive engagement. Every religious tradition, with its own heritage and resources, is called upon to propose a vision of the public, even while each tradition is motivated to be engaged with others to envision a common public.

Public theology treats politics, the site where public decisions are made, as its important arena of involvement. It theologizes publicly on public dimensions of human living like the nature of the State, democracy, economics, market, society, civil society, bureaucracy, public policies, public institutions, public issues, cultural institutions, and public life. By so doing, it embarks upon a highly challenging path which 'involves' in politics without however seeking to establish itself at the level of a constitutionally democratic State.[8]

Its modus operandi is *conversation* on public policies and means to achieve common good. It means that we begin to reflect upon public issues from the perspective of faith, and that we consider Christianity, with all its denominational variants together ('communion of communion') as a 'public church' in relation to other religions, ideologies, and statecraft.

Becoming effective agents of mission in the public means 'joining in with the Spirit of God' at the public sphere. Rowan Williams said it well on Christian mission as 'finding out where the Holy Spirit is at work and joining in'. The well-known *Missio Dei* mission paradigm exhorted us that mission is the Church joining in with the initiative of the Triune God – the Father sending the Son and the Spirit to redeem and reconcile the creation with God's own self. From within this Trinitarian mission paradigm, today, going by the 'signs of the time', we are called upon to 'join in' with the Spirit of God who discloses God's self to us. As the Spirit of God 'blows where S/He wills' (Jn 3:8), by going beyond boundaries, we too need to cross the boundaries to 'join in' with the Spirit of God. Public is

---

7 It's a phrase from John Rawls to stand for the religio-ethical doctrines which give a comprehensive explanation of reality.

8 It is in place to quote Charles Davis, who, speaking about theology and political society says: "political society expresses its faith in the transcendent by its refusal to establish an official religion" – Charles Davis, *Theology and Political Society* (New York: Cambridge University Press, 1980), 20.

that space beyond boundaries, and public theology[9] is the light with which we search for the Spirit of God in that space.

It is in place to recall here the fact that the early Christian and the patristic era presented mission as a command to continue to actualise the self-communication/revelation of God that occurred in Jesus Christ. Preserving the fullness of this revelation and passing it on effectively to successive generations became a major concern of mission. The Reformation era presented mission as proclaiming the self-communication of God here and now to the believer. Rather than remembering a past, actualising a present (here and now) gifted by God became the major concern of the Reforming mission. Continuing along these orientations upon the past and the present, our mission today has an eschatological orientation, and it is the Spirit of God, who leads us towards this future. One remembers the prediction of the mystic Joachim of Fiore (1135-1202) that the future is going to be an era of the Holy Spirit.

9 It must be noted here that this initiative of doing public theology is already prevalent in countries like South Africa, UK, USA, Korea, Germany, etc. It is now being introduced to the Indian context, where many critical questions are already being raised upon it. A very common question is 'what is different in public theology from liberation-contextual theologies?' What liberation theology spoke in terms of socio-political and economic liberation, public theology seems to repeat, and so, what is the difference between the two? My answer, very succinctly, would be 'that which constitutes our global world makes the difference'. Liberation theology and its variants of contextual theologies emerged in a context prior to the advancement of the global world, and their audiences were typically the Christians; but today, we want every religious or secular community to make liberation their ideal, and therefore the need of proposing a public liberation–contextual theology. Another associated question is, 'does public theology not emerge from the erstwhile political theology, which was named by Latin American liberation theologians as the bourgeois theology of the rich'? Again, my short answer would be, 'politics is not any more the domain of the bourgeois, and people's politics needs to be revolutionized in an important way today'. A public theology, as undertaken from the Indian context will be at once contextual and public, and therefore, we could pursue a 'subaltern public theology'. Another question that comes from philosophically oriented people is: 'is it not an aspect of the post-modern trend today?' Perhaps, it needs a longer answer: public theology is both post-modern and modern in its philosophical underpinnings. It does not get satisfied with the post-modern understanding of reality as fragments, though it does, along with the post-modernists, question the eternal validity of universal meta-narratives. It envisions to bring about an interactive, inter-subjective universality between the *fragments* so as to be able to hold a public opinion in a global world. In addition, it believes in the need of a transcendental referent for our public life, be it in its political, economic, social, cultural, familial aspects. Yet another important question could be, 'can public theology proposed by Christians in India, a minority population, be really public?', 'does it not suit countries which are predominantly Christian?' My answer would be: countries are increasingly becoming multi-religious, and no country can assume power over the public due to the salience of one particular religion; in the Indian context too, we are acutely becoming aware of the multi-religiosity of our country, and precisely in such a context that public theology, which is inter-religious and ecumenical, becomes meaningful and necessary.

## 2. Opening the Public by the Spirit of God

Spirit of God opens the public transformatively so that every form of life (nature, humans, and life other than humans), especially that which gets subjugated through the manipulations of the dominant, *participates in the public conversation* and experiences the creative, redemptive, and accompanying presence of the Spirit of God. The public is the meeting point of different individuals and collective / institutional others, to mediate life and freedom. Meeting points, unfortunately, are infected today with the sinfulness of the created reality, as evident in its intransigence and closure towards the future and towards different others. Social, psychological, cultural, political and economic factors which initiate and maintain such closures are forms of exclusions, accumulations, deprivations, and, discriminations. At the root of these closures are the historical mutations of the evil spirit, the embodiment of fear and insecurity in the face of the other.

Spirit of the living God initiates us into the public, by gracefully opening the public for us. S/he opens the shutters – social, cultural, religious, political and economic – which exclude the marginalised from the public. S/he, with Her/His prophetic promptings, interrogates the hegemonic closures imposed on the public on the one hand, and, with Her/His indwelling presence, enables (empowers) us to partake of the public, on the other. S/he gifts Her/His indwelling presence in a public through multiple mediations, the religio-cultural traditions of the subaltern people being an important one at that.

This presence of the Spirit of God initiates a radical openness not merely to eternity, but to the future of the historical time. As Jürgen Moltmann put it, 'this presence of the Spirit is the presence of future glory, which fulfils the times; it is not the presence of eternity, which obliterates time altogether... this experience does not snatch people out of time but makes them open for time's future'.[10] History, somtimes, has tempted or tempting us to be pinned down to the past and selfishly glued to the immediate present. The Enlightenment modernity has contributed its share to the human experience of being lost in the immediate present. That, of all the millennia when human beings have lived on this earth, the past three-four modern centuries have contributed to the vandalising of the eco-system is a case in point. The instrumental rationality, when pushed to an extreme, spreads the sinful spirit of narrow immediacy. Spirit of God motivates us to open ourselves, our consciousness in particular to the future.

The opening, again, is a radical motivation to emerge out of self-centredness to go out to meet with the multiple, strange others at the public. This horizontal opening towards the historical others is a dynamic act which keeps overcoming multiple barriers on the way. The contemporary world presents us with the hurdles of fundamentalism based on religio-cultural and social identities. It is,

10 Jürgen Moltmann, *The Trinity and the Kingdom – The Doctrine of God* (Minneapolis: Fortress Press, 1993 [1981]), pp. 124-125.

then, the Spirit of God who expands our hearts and structures, and enables us to open the public from these fundamentalisms. Moses experienced this Spirit of God when he refused, on the complaint from Joshua, to stop Eldad and Medad from prophesying, saying, 'Would that all the people of the Lord were prophets! Would that the Lord might bestow his spirit on them all!' (Num 11:27-29). The well-known pneumatological text of Joel 2:28-29, speaking about 'pouring out the spirit on all flesh - sons, daughters, young, old, male, female,' gives a universal outreach to the realm of the Spirit and it resonates well with the open public. This openness is a singular gift of the Spirit of God specially meant for public life. Jesus, upon being anointed by the Holy Spirit, initiated a proclamation to open the public to the poor, captives, blind, and the oppressed (Lk 4:16-19). Paul, led by the Spirit, mediated the offer of salvation to the 'gentiles', and stoutly defended it. These openings of the Spirit of God continue in history today in and through individuals, organisations, movements, and ideologies which struggle to open the public for all creation of God.

## 3. Doing the Public Theology of Mission

It is with this faith in the Spirit of God that we do a public theology of mission. Following are some areas of this theology:

### 3.1 Strengthening of Indian Democracy

Wherever there is creative and healthy public theology, there will also emerge a healthy system of democracy. India is yet to mature as a country with a substantive form of democracy. According to a democracy audit of countries across the globe,[11] India comes at the 51st position, leaving much to be desired.

Christianity has been a major player in bringing Indian democracy to birth. Starting with its contribution in ensuing an Indian renaissance by bringing to light the Indian classical religio-cultural and philosophical heritage, with its contribution to the 'silent revolution' of the subaltern classes of people by educating and imparting awareness of civil and human rights to them, with its contribution to the post-independent nation-building, and with its solidarity with the poor and the marginalised for their economic and social empowerment, Christianity has indeed played a significant role in nurturing the ideals of democracy. Needless to say that Indian Christianity has contributed also to the emergence of a public sphere in India by way of introducing the print media, and then being present emphatically in the contemporary media world. These contributions make Indian Christianity even more responsible for the continuing growth of Indian democracy, inspite of the fact that Christianity is only a minority religion in India.

Evangelical Christianity is one of the fastest growing religion in India. What will be the relationship between this Christianity and democracy in India is an

11 http://www.worldaudit.org/democracy.htm

important question for public theology today. There are scholars who argue for the suitability of evangelical Christianity for the democratic processes.[12] David Lumsdaine, for example, opines that, "the embrace of evangelical Christianity has often enabled poor and marginalized people to have greater prosperity, self-confidence, and civic skills and a more vital associational life and has consequently pushed societies toward more open and democratic processes."[13] Evangelical Christianity, as an heightened form of Protestantism, bases itself solely upon the Biblical revelation, thus democratising the sphere of Christian faith, enabling every individual, regardless of her / his ascriptive ties, practise Christianity on her / his own. This possibility of receiving the biblical revelation individually, legitimated with special gifts of the Spirit, contributes to the emergence of individual agency in societal relationships, and this motivates the individual to participate in the public sphere, resulting in the strengthening of democracy.

However, an important aspect of evangelical Christianity is persuasion in mission, which might ensue in conflicts with other religious traditions in the public sphere. And, again, the evangelical Christianity goes well with the rising middle classes, and can therefore serve the needs of these people, forgetting the disparities being created by the market-led world in economic, educational, and employment opportunities. Democracy cannot be meaningful if it is creating newer forms of disparities and exclusions. Thus, what is given with one hand by evangelical Christianity to the process of democracy seems to be taken back with the other hand. All these concerns associated with the relationship of evangelical Christianity to democracy need be understood and responded to theologically with effective public theologies.

## 3.2 Mission as a Public Conversation

Christian mission needs to present its project as a public statement. It presents its vision of transforming the contemporary society, characterised by multiple sinful closures, to become a society that can experience the Divine mystery, by way of opening itself up to a life of freedom. In presenting this vision, it announces its faith in the Divine Grace that comes through the person and message of Jesus Christ. While doing so, it beseeches God to give it the humility and openness to free itself from obstacles of triumphalism and assumption of superiority of truth. Its claim on a unique revelation, it believes, can be publicly communicated and discussed meaningfully.

Mission, thus, becomes a public 'conversation'. When we undertake this public conversation, say in a church, or in an academic circle, or in a civil society group or in a platform of the political society, we follow the virtues of genuine conversations. Without getting stuck with fideism, for example, we become

12 Cf. David Halloran Lumsdaine, *Evangelical Christianity and Democracy in Asia* (New York: Oxford University Press, 2009).

13 Ibid., p. 3.

confident of expressing our faith in the public. As Max Stackhouse puts it: "[A] public theology ... differs from those forms of fideism that assert purportedly universal and absolute beliefs on the basis of a presumed infallibility of one or another tradition's scripture, or on the basis of any materialist fundamentalism or humanistic metaphysic that denies the possibility that transcendence could or should be the resource in life or thought."[14]

## 3.3 Mission as Making Christian Values Public

A public theology of mission proposes to the wider public the meaningfulness of Christian values found in their scriptures and tradition. Christianity, for example, has been privileging all through its history the value of service to humanity as an integral part of its faith. Christianity in India has been endeavouring genuinely to render this service to the people of India.

How does the wider public respond to this? Has it duly acknowledged this service? It is quite perceptive of Felix Wilfred to point out to the fact that the caste-based consciousness of the Indian society might treat the Christian service to others as nothing but the caste-based duty of the Christian *shudra* and the *servile* classes to serve others.[15] It means that the Christian service is not appreciated for its faith-based value, but only for fulfilling a caste-based *dharma*, which is but incumbent upon them. This not only belittles, but also de-radicalises the Christian vision of service. Service to the subalterns, as part of our vision, is nothing short of aiming at the total liberation of humanity from its bondages. It would imply, in the Indian context, the liberation specifically from bondages imposed by the sinful system of caste. The Indian contextual Dalit theology has brought out this point very poignantly to the Indian Christian mind. It is time that Christianity endeavours to bring this point to the Indian mind as well.

## 3.4 Mission as Making Public Values Christian

It is not merely in giving, but also in receiving that public mission obtains its significance. Christianity in India needs to make some of the authentic values of the public its own. For example, democracy is the best of public value that an open society endeavours to cultivate. Church needs to cultivate this value of democracy within its inner space too. Participation of the members of the Church in its decision-making process is a dire necessity for the recognition of the Church as a public person. The long-standing imbalance of power between laity and clergy, men and women, rich and poor, etc., with closures along the lines of caste, language, and region should be rectified in order for the Church to become a public institution. By way of nurturing the inner democracy, the Church should

---

14 Max L. Stackhouse, *God and Globalization – Globalization and Grace,* Vol. 4 (New York: Continuum, 2007), 78.

15 Cf. Felix Wilfred, *Christians for a Better India* (New Delhi: ISPCK, 2014), 72ff.

promote the growth of public sphere within its body too. Public sphere is the space where discussions and debates take place in an atmosphere of freedom of opinion. The Church needs to form several fora where such discussions and debates can take place. Growth of such fora will have direct bearing upon the quality of public sphere, and eventually upon the quality of democracy practised within the Church.

Church, in the era of public mission, must place itself also under economic, ethical and other important forms of auditing from independent agencies. Shedding its image of being a pampered organisation under the cover of charitable organisation, it must submit itself to external auditing of its financial accounts; by way of evaluating its moral standards, it must submit itself to ethical auditing to see whether it is genuinely committed to the values and objectives that it stands for; by way of reviewing the efficient management of human resources, it must submit itself for an auditing in this regard too; and, by way of evaluating its impact upon the wider society, it must undertake a social auditing as well. The list can be many more. By applying all these forms of auditing, the Church will emerge as a public organ, through a process of maturing in transparency and public interactions.

The leadership of the Church will have to grow more steadily in the public value of democracy. Those who occupy leadership positions must regularly update themselves in leadership skills and qualities, and improve upon their standard of performance. Those that cannot perform, should have the humility to leave the opportunities to others.

## 3.5 Public Sphere as the Site of Public Mission

Public theology of mission cannot be pursued without the availability of a public sphere, a domain which lives in discursive practices like dialogue, conversation, contestation, interrogation, negotiation, and so on. Generally it is the civil society where such practices take place. To the extent these practices are effective, to that extent they transform the social systems for better freedom, equality, dignity, and well-being. There is no gainsaying the fact that historically Christianity contributed significantly to the emergence of a discursive public, by introducing the printing press, publication of classics, imparting modern education to the wider public, etc. A historic contribution worthy of Indian Christianity is that it has enabled a section of the subaltern people of India to gain the ability to participate in the discursive public sphere of India. However, the strength of this contribution seems to weaken today: the political sphere, media space, educational sphere, bureaucracy, and other public systems have come to be dominated by the 'dominant' sections of the people of India. It is indeed a challenge to empower the subalterns to participate in the contemporary public sphere, especially with their agenda for social justice.

## 4. Some Salient Issues

### 4.1 Issue of Religious Conversion in India

Religious Conversion has been a perennial issue confronting Christians in the Indian context. Right from the time of the missionary era, conflict and controversies have abounded in this regard. However, the more recent and the contemporary eras have added their own specific dimensions too. The phenomenon of nationalism, a political child of modernity, has engulfed the debate in a paralysing manner. Nationalist leaders and organisations of various hues have found fault with conversion, treating it as a 'de-nationalising' force among Indians. Gandhi, the pioneering political nationalist, said, 'If I had power and could legislate, I would outlaw proselytising.'[16] Some provincial States went so far as to legislate upon anti-conversion laws right at the dawn of the Republic of India, fearing that the Scheduled Castes and Tribes of India would convert to Christianity. The amendments made to Hindu personal laws by *The Hindu Marriage Act (1955)* made inheritance of property by converts impossible, and the Presidential Order of 1950 denied the benefits of reservation to Christians of Scheduled Caste origin by way of restraining the Hindus from converting.

The contemporary era has given salience to religio-cultural nationalism as a framework for the practice of democracy in India, and this has resulted in the emergence of the Hindu Right with its majoritarian politics. While majority of Hindus have fewer problems with religious conversion per se, the Hindu Right which is posing as the representative of Hinduism provokes controversies and conflicts. It needs be noted, however, that a feeble voice among the Hindu Right demand 'debate' upon conversion, while the majority of the Hindu Right harbour grudge against it, and inflict violence upon Christians, their places of worship and religious symbols. The magnitude of such violence keeps rising year by year.

Christians respond in various ways to violent incidents related to conversion. They show their solidarity with the victims of violence by visiting them; They mobilise economic support necessary for re-building the lives of the victims; They make representations to civil and political authorities to ameliorate the conditions of the victims; They demonstrate publicly against the violence done to them; They organise various initiatives for bringing back inter-religious amity in the locality of violence; They take legal course of actions to seek protection under the 'freedom of religion' clause of the Constitution; and so on. These ways have become the general pattern of responding to violence related to conversion. Such responses are necessary and effective in the immediate context. Along with these incident-specific responses, Indian Christians need to think also of those which make long-term impact too. Say, for example, entering into the civil sphere more

16 Cited in Bhagwan Josh, "Conversion, Complicity, and the State in Post-Independent India," in *Christianity and the State in Asia – Complicity and Conflict*, eds. Julius Bautista and Francis Khek Gee Lim (New York: Routledge, 2009), 97.

actively to arrest the emergence of fundamentalism of various hues would be a substantive way of doing public theology.

## 4.2 'Freedom of Religion'

One of the important concerns of public theology in the Indian context is the interpretation of the 'freedom of religion' clause in the Indian Constitution, a clause closely associated with the issue of conversion. The clause, adopted from similar rights given in the Universal Declaration of Human Rights, reads as: 'Subject to public order, morality and health ..., all persons are equally entitled to freedom of conscience and the right freely to profess, practise and propagate religion' (Art. 25. 1). The bone of contention in this clause is the word "propagate", which was introduced into the Constitution after much debate in the Constituent Assembly.[17] While there should be no problem for the private "professing and practising" of religion, it would become a real issue when it comes to the right of propagation, which is a public activity. As noted above, some provincial governments sought to protect themselves against the implications of the clause by legislating upon anti-conversion laws, attaching such pejorative motives as 'fraud, coercion", etc.

We need to discuss the meaning of the freedom of religion clause in a new context today. We need, first of all, to ask the broader question of the relevance and meaningfulness of this clause to a democratic system of politics. The core question is 'whether democracy stands to gain or lose when the Indian citizen exercises her / his right to propagate in the right and genuine sense her / his religion?' Any mature democracy should respect the freedom of conscience to choose one's religion, practise it, and even propagate it, without causing problem to law, order and public morality. Indian Christianity needs to work towards protecting this freedom and help democracy mature. Public theology will continue to shed light upon the meaningfulness of this clause in varying contexts.

## 4.3 Relationship with Other Religions

Relationship of Christianity with other religions has been a perennial issue in the Indian context. For a long time in history, it had been informed by various theologies of religions. Starting with the classical exclusivism, Christianity in India has endeavoured to practice inclusive and even pluralist approaches at various phases of history. What has been the salient element in these phases is an initial projection of a statement of truth regarding other religions, and then endeavouring to follow it meaningfully. Indian Christianity has bothered less to listen to others on their views of other religions, and concerned more to present their own stances to others.

---

17 Cf. Sebastian Kim, *In Search of Identity – Debates on Religious Conversion in India* (New Delhi: Oxford University Press, 2003).

The dynamics of public theology demands that Christians relate with other religions interactively and inter-subjectively. The truth of Christianity needs be tested in the public arena, in multiple acts of public conversations. The most relevant form of conversation is forging an embodied relationship with others. It is in being involved in actual forms of relationships with people of other faiths, that Christians will evince respect and understanding towards others. An effective way of being involved in such relationships is serving as a catalyst to bring together multiple others (religions) in various networking for common good.

## 4.4 Living with Minority Identity and Rights

It is a well-known fact that Christians in India preferred the minority rights to communal representation in the post-independent Indian parliament. Christian leaders were more concerned about ensuring the religio-cultural rights of Christians even while foregoing the opportunity to send representatives to the legislature. Minority rights, they thought, would enable the Christians to cultivate their religio-cultural traditions and live with them.

Living with minority rights has come under serious strains today. Religio-cultural nationalism, relentlessly pursued by the majoritarian political forces, is choking, ignoring, and even antagonising the religio-cultural traditions of the minorities. History is being re-written at several nodal points to impose a history that suits the majoritarian politics; religio-cultural traditions of the minorities are not given their due place in the educational stream; historical monuments of the minorities are being erased or replaced with other monuments.

These suffocating experiences of the minorities bring back the question of the need of their voice being heard in the legislature, the political decision-making body. This is one of the salient concerns that the Indian public theology of mission will have to grapple with. While Indian Christianity does not want to become sectarian in any sense of the term, it also needs to legitimately voice out its concerns in proper fora and get them redressed. For example, recently, the Chennai edition of the Deccan Chronicle dt. 4 Oct 2015, carried a news item with the caption, "Many undertrials belong to Islam, Christianity". The content read that,

> 'according to the National Crime Record Bureau, almost one in two undertrials in Tamil Nadu belongs to either Muslims or Christian communities. Though Christians and Muslims comprise 6.12 per cent and 5.86 per cent of the state's total population, the two communities together account for about 48 per cent of the undertrials in the state. Of the total 9,034 undertrials, Muslims and Christians comprise 1,867 and 2,538 prisoners respectively. Mr. A. Kathir, executive director of Evidence, said that this data indicate the presence of discrimination in law enforcement.'

Needless to say this is very shocking to the minority communities in Tamil Nadu; it is indeed an alarm to minorities all over India. Question is 'How to account for such a data'? Are Christians and Muslims more criminal than others in Tamil Nadu? One always thought that at least the Christians who have benefitted much out of the educational system would be more civilised and less criminal than others. But the data implicate precisely the Christians! Is there any agenda of criminalisation involved? Sad thing is no one has reacted or commented upon it. How to get this right?

## 5. Concluding Remarks

The event of Christian mission has journeyed through various stages in history, acquiring various shades of meaning and implications. Signs of the times today give us a call to join in with the Spirit of God at the public sphere.

Public theology of mission primarily is a response to the presence of the Spirit of God in the public sphere, where conversations between religions, ethical doctrines, ideologies, systems and movements take place beyond narrow boundaries. It arises generally at the interface between civil and political spheres within the framework of democracy.

Doing a public theology of mission would then mean strengthening the bonds of democracy in a given political system, and treating the public sphere as the site of mission; it would mean presenting our values to the public, and conversely, imbibing some of the pristine values of the public; it would mean standing for the fundamental rights provided by democratic systems; it would mean networking with other religions and movements for common good; etc. It would ultimately mean joining in with the Spirit of God who opens the sinful closures of the public so that the public can mediate life in freedom for the whole of creation.

## Bibliography

Atherton, John. *Public Theology for Changing Times.* GB: SPCK, 2000.

Forrester, Duncan B. "Lesslie Newbigin as Public Theologian," in *A Scandalous Prophet – The Way of Mission after Newbigin*, ed. by Thomas F. Foust, *et al*, 3-12. Grand Rapids, MI: William B. Eerdmans Publishing Company, 2002.

Foust, Thomas F. et al (eds). *A Scandalous Prophet – The Way of Mission after Newbigin.* Grand Rapids, MI: William B. Eerdmans Publishing Company, 2002.

Hogan, Linda, et. al. eds. *From World Mission to Inter-Religious Witness*, Concilium, 2011/1.

Shahan, Michael (ed). *A Report from the Front Lines – Conversations on Public Theology.* (A Festschrift in houour of Robert Benne). Grand Rapids, MI: William B. Eerdmans Publishing Company, 2009.

Soares-Prabhu, George, *Biblical Themes For a Contextual Theology Today*, Collected Writings of George M. Soares-Prabhu, Vol. 1. Pune: JDV, 1999.

Stackhouse, Max L. "How and Why We Go Public?," in *Transforming Praxis, God, Community and Church*, edited by C.I. David Joy, 36-46. New Delhi: ISPCK, 2008.

_________________ *God and Globalization – Globalization and Grace*, Vol. 4, New York: Continuum, 2007.

_________________ *Public Theology and Political Economy*. USA: Wm. B. Eerdmans Publishing Co., 1987.

Stackhouse, Max L with Don S. Browning (eds). *The Spirit and the Modern Authorities*. Pennsylvannia: Trinity Press International, 2001.

Stackhouse, Max L with Peter J. Paris (eds). *God and Globalization – Religion and the Powers of the Common Life*, Vol. 1. Pennsylvania: Trinity Press International, 2000.

Storrar, William F. and Andrew R. Morton (eds). *Public Theology for the 21st Century*. London: T & T Clark, 2004.

Wilfred, Felix. *Christians for a Better India*. New Delhi: ISPCK, 2014.

*Chapter 5*

# FULFILLING THE GREAT COMMISSION IN A MULTI-FAITH CONTEXT

Jacob Kurian[1]

Although we are tempted to avoid the term 'mission', the missiological significance of our Christian identity, prompts time and again to think seriously about fulfilling the great Commission of our Lord, in our multi-faith context. Moreover, a missiological re-consideration of our task is necessitated by the fragmentising factors of the multi-faith context, like the 'IS' threat, jargons like love-jihad and 'ghar wapasi; etc.

## 1. What is Significant in the Great Commission?

The factual veracity of a final commissioning by the Risen Lord is testified in the gospels and the Acts of Apostles (Matt. 28:18-20, Mk. 16:14-18, Lk. 24:36-49, Jn. 20:19-23, Acts 1:6-8). Obviously it becomes the Great Commission to reach out **to all peoples and to the ends of the earth**. The earlier commissioning of the twelve and the seventy was more or less confined to the ministry to the jews of Palestine and Diaspora. Therefore, the significant thing in the great commission is its addressing the *pluralistic context*, more specifically *the multi-faith context.* "The flow of people with their religious identities from the South to the North and from the North to the South, resurgence of religion in conservative forms, increasing

1 Fr. Dr. Jacob Kurian is a Professor Emeritus & Former Principal of the Orthodox Theological Seminary, Kottayam.

instances of violence in the name of religion, proliferation of new religious movements etc. have contributed to an awareness of religious plurality as a global context". (Jacob Kurian, "Being Christian neigbhours in the context of religious plurality: certain theological considerations", F & O Plenary Presentation, Kaula Lumpur, Malaysia, 28 July – 6 August 2004).

## 2. The Multi-Faith Context: Change in Attitudes

"Religiously homogenous societies are being replaced by multi-religious societies. Now that religions are living in permanent and close interaction with each other, religious plurality is no longer a conceptual issue, it affects the very texture of societal life and creates now paradigms, new multi-relationships and multiple belonging within our institutions, our families and even within ourselves" (H. H. Aram I, Report of the Moderator, WCC Central Committee, 26 August-2 September 2003). The Multi-Faith context, manifested in variegated forms, has witnessed different attitudes on the way of fulfilling the Great Commission. Christianity in the midst of persecution struggled a lot to survive with an attitude of *peaceful co-existence and courageous witnessing*. Christianity when assumed the status of 'Royal' Religion displayed an uneasiness to the "others" and developed a 'conquest' or 'transplantation' attitude that continued down through centuries till the emergence of "younger" churches in Asia and Africa. When the western missionary enterprise advanced to Asia and Africa under the protection of Colonisation, the issue of the faith-forms and cultures of the local people became crucial. Gradually, there occurred a change of attitude at different levels, particularly on the part of missionaries, scholars and converts. The multi-faith context became a serious issue for study and debate in close connection with the modern ecumenical movement.

## 3. Fulfilling the Great Commission: Ecumenical Discussions

From the very beginning of the modern ecumenical movement, there had been two streams of western Christianity collaborating, viz., the evangelical missionary stream and the church-unity stream. These two streams known as the 'evangelicals' and the 'ecumenicals' carried with them a corresponding priority in their agenda, the former emphasising Christian unity for *Christian revival and missionary advance,* while the latter emphasising Christian-unity for *world-peace and social action.* 'Evangelicals' and 'Ecumenicals' when came together in conferences attempted to push their respective agendas. And this had very clear expression in their discussions on Christian message in Multi Faith Contexts.

As early as the World Missionary Conference at Edinburgh (1910), the issue of other faiths in relation to Christian message was raised by people like J. N. Farquhar and it was further seriously discussed at the next conference at Jerusalem (1928). The Tambaram Missionary Conference (1938) opened a debate over the significance of other faiths and cultures. Henri Kraemer's Keynote address at Tambaram on "Christian message in a non-Christian world" and the subsequent debate, manifested the tension between the unique and the universal aspects of Christian message. In the first WCC Assembly at Amsterdam (1948), the challenge of the younger churches to reckon with the truth-claims of non-Christian religions was brought to special attention by such Asian leaders like P. D. Devanandan. Following the Evanston Assembly (1954) which noted with special interest the fact of 'the renaissance of non-Christian religions', the WCC launched a special study process on "the Word of God and the living Faiths of Men". In his address entitled "Called to Witness" at the New Delhi Assembly of WCC (1961), Devanandan invited Christians for 'dialogue' with other religions to project Jesus Christ as the Light of the World. Consultations under the auspices of WCC at Jerusalem, Nagpur, Hongkong, Rangoon, Kandy, Ajaltoun, Zurich etc and the subsequent WCC Assemblies brought to light the missiological and theological significance of Dialogue with living faiths and ideologies. However, the 'dialogue'-trend promoted by the WCC's Sub-Unit on Dialogue had to face opposition from the conservative evangelical and Orthodox circles which had a fear of "syncretism".

## 4. The Great Commission, the Challenging Context and the Roman Catholic Church

In the Roman Catholic Church, a clear change in the attitude to the non-Christian religions was brought by Vatican II (1962-64). Vatican II encouraged the Catholic faithful to co-operate "prudently and lovingly through dialogue and collaboration with other religions". In 1964, Pope Paul VI instituted the Secretariat for Non-Christians. National Bishops' Commissions were set up for dialogue with other religions. In India, the CBCI Commission for Dialogue brought out a document in 1977 called "Guidelines for inter-religious Dialogue."

## 5. The New Christological, Theological and Missiological Trends

Emerging openness to the multi-faith context had its immediate signs in Christological and Theological reflections. John Hick and others envisaged a **Copernican Revolution** in Christological and Theological understandings. **Christocentric** Theology was exhorted to be transformed as **Theocentric Christology.** The universal significance of Christ beyond the boundaries of the historical church was hinted at in such terms and phrases like "hidden", "unknown", "acknowledged", 'unbound', 'anonymous' etc. New Missiological approaches like, 'Fulfilment', 'Translation', 'Dialogue', 'Synthesis', 'Praxis' etc. became popular. In place of the old paradigms of "exclusivism", new paradigms of "inclusivism", "pluralism", "inclusive-pluralism" and "pluralistic inclusivism" found attention.

In summary, there emerged three main issues in relation to the Great Commission in a multi-faith context:

(a) The salvific significance of other faiths
(b) The role and significance of other faiths for peace, justice and the integrity of creation
(c) The rationale and methodology of a missiological approach to the multi-faith context.

## 6. From W. C. C "Guidelines" till "Self-Understanding"

The above mentioned three issues together or independently were focussed in a series of documents, conferences, reports and studies from 1979 till 2006. A random selection of seven of them in citations will speak for themselves:

### (a) Guidelines on Dialogue with People of Living Faiths and Ideologies (1979)

(This W.C.C document was "revisited" in 2003 and published under the title 'Ecumenical Considerations')

"In dialogue and relationships with people of other faiths, we have come to recognize that the mystery of God's salvation is not exhausted by our theological affirmations. Salvation belongs to God. We therefore dare not stand in judgement of others. While witnessing to our own faith, we seek to understand the ways in which God intends to bring God's purposes to their fulfilment" (para 17).

### (b) San Antonio (WME) Report (1989)

"In reaffirming the 'evangelistic mandate' of the ecumenical movement, we would like to emphasize that we may never claim to have a full understanding of God's truth: we are only the recipients of God's grace. Our ministry of witness among people of other faiths presupposes our **presence** faith commitments and experiences, **willingness** to be their servants for Christ's sake, **affirmation** of what God has done and is doing among them, and **love** for them.....

We cannot point to any other way of salvation than Jesus Christ, at the same time we cannot set limits to the saving power of God...." (paras 25, 26).

### (c) Theological Perspectives on Plurality: WCC Consultation, Baar, Switzerland (1990)

"We also affirm that the Holy Spirit, the Interpreter of Christ and of our own scriptures (Jn. 14:26) will lead us to understand afresh the deposit of the faith already given to us, and into fresh and unexpected discovery of new wisdom and insight, as we learn more from our neighbours of other faiths" (Section IV).

## (d) Canberra Assembly (1991)

As a continuation of the controversies at the Nairobi (1975) and Vancouver (1983) Assemblies, the W.C.C. Assembly at Canberra precipitated the debate over the ways and nature of the function of the Holy Spirit in other cultures and religions. Some of the evangelicals and the Orthodox alleged "syncretism" in the ecumenical approaches to the multi-faith context, and it effected a 'check' on the enthusiasm for inter-religious dialogue. "It is this context of a clash between an assimilative globalization and a fragmenting struggle for particularity that constitutes the locus of missio Dei to-day" (Dr. Christopher Duraisingh, "Mission towards reconciled and inter-contextual communities", IRM, Vol. XCI, No. 363, October 2002, p. 487).

## (e) Dominus Iesus (2000)

The declaration entitled 'Dominus Iesus' on the unity and salvific universality of Jesus Christ and the Church, by the Congregation (R. Catholic) for the Doctrine of Faith, attempted to give clarity to the issue of Christians in their relation to other faiths. (It is to be explored whether it gave 'clarity' or it created 'confusion'!) Although it declared that, "the salvific action of Jesus Christ, with and through his Spirit, extends beyond the visible boundaries of the Church to all humanity", it firmly projected the Church as the "universal sacrament of salvation". The church has the definite task of "proclaiming to all people the truth definitively revealed by the Lord" and "announcing the necessity of conversion to Jesus Christ and of adherence to the Church through Baptism and other sacraments". Dominus Iesus, thus, limited the inter-religious dialogue as part of Church's evangelizing mission. It further, dismissed an attitude of mutual complementary roles in Christian-non-Christian relations: "Therefore, the theory of the limited, incomplete, or imperfect character of the revelation of Jesus Christ, which would be complementary to that found in other religions, is contrary to the Church's faith. Such a position would claim to be based on the notion that the truth about God cannot be grasped and manifested in its globality and completeness by any historical religion, neither by Christianity nor by Jesus Christ".

## (f) W.C.C. Moderator's (Central Committee Report (2003)

The then W.C.C. Moderator, H. H. Aram I, made an epoch making observation at the August-September session (2003) of the Central Committee. Pointing that 21st century will become "the age of religion", the Moderator observed the necessity of "living our faith and proclaiming Christ in pluralistic communities", taking "the opportunity" to dialogue and witness with other faiths: "Christian mission is rooted in God's salvific act. God's saving work transcends the Church's boundaries and reveals itself in history in manifold ways. Religions respond to God's offer of salvation in quite different ways as well. An inclusive understanding of God's salvific act will lead the church to consider other religions as part of God's plan of salvation and not as mere 'mission fields'. In our missionary strategy we should not, particularly in pluralistic environments, seek to add new members, rather we should seek to identify the Church values in other religions and awaken the Christ who sleeps in the night of the religions" (section 3).

### (g) "Religious Plurality and Christian Self-Understanding" (2006)

According to the decision of the W.C.C. Central Committee, three streams of the WCC (Faith and Order, World Mission and Evangelism, Inter-Religious Relation) jointly worked out a document entitled "Religious Plurality and Christian Self-Understanding". This document was presented to the WCC Assembly at Porto-Alegre (2006). There are at least four facts in the document that are significant for fulfilling the Great Commission in a multi-faith context:

- (i) Religious traditions of human kind in their diversity are **journeys** or **pilgrimages** towards the fullness of truth (para 44).
- (ii) A paradigm shift from 'dialogue' to "hospitality in humility and mutuality" is required in inter-religious relation (para 26).
- (iii) No human claim, articulation, experience or conviction can claim to have grasped the fullness of the Mystery of Salvation in God's plan (para 46).
- (iv) Christian mission is basically an openness to be 'hosts' and 'guests' at the same time, in sharing the ongoing God's Mission revealed in Jesus Christ and guided by the Holy Spirit (para 37).

## 7. The Text and the Context in Contemporary Times

### (a) The Text

There are four segments in the great commission as embodied in Matt 28:18-20.

- (i) Go to all peoples everywhere
- (ii) Make them disciples
- (iii) Baptize them
- (iv) Teach them

The text can be expounded mainly in two perspectives, viz., **'the Church-growth'-perspective** and **the 'discipleship'-perspective.** A 'Church-growth' perspective can interpret the Great Commission as a direct commandment for quantitative expansion of the Church through conversion and baptism. But the New Testament witness does not fully subscribe to an intention on the part of Jesus to build up an organisational project with an initiation-rite called baptism. On the other hand, a 'discipleship-perspective' can have a qualitative understanding of 'discipleship', being extended to all peoples everywhere with a symbolic significance to baptism. It is possible that 'discipleship' could be a 'movement' with different levels of its crystalisation, from that of a historical organisation to that of a spiritual and invisible fellowship (consisting even 'anonymous' membership).

### (b) The Context

The Great Commandment can be summarised in the context of the entire New Testament as call for "mission", "witnessing" and "discipleship". Mission, witnessing and discipleship in contemporary context have to recognise the positive and unitive challenge of the growing multi-faith interaction in a global living. This positive challenge can be called 'fraternisation', through peaceful-co-existence and meaningful participation for justice, peace and the integrity of creation. Fraternization is also self-denying and cross-bearing witnessing of Christ's love on the part of Christians to which Mother Teresa, Graham Stanes and Sister Rani Maria and many martyrs of Kandamal (India), etc., testify.

On the other hand, the contemporary context frightens us with a negative and divisive threat of 'fragmentisation'. "Fragmentisation" in the multi-faith context expresses itself through blind conservatism in religion, militant fundamentalism, religious nationalism and politicization of religion. The 'IS' threat, 'Love-Jihad', 'Ghar-wapasi', etc., are only few signs of such forces in action.

## 8. Brief Comment on the Islamic and Hindu Fundamentalist Tendencies

### (a) 'IS' Threat and Global Islamic Expansion

'IS' (Islamic State) campaign to establish an Islamic Rule over the world is assuming fierce forms through ISIS (Islamic State of Iraq and Syria), ISIL (Islamic State of Iraq and Levant), etc. Incidents of violence and recruitment of hostage-volunteers in various parts of the world including India cannot be ignored. This has been backed by the "salafi" ideology of "loyalty to everything considered Islam and disavowal of everything not Islam". 'IS' threat carries with it five major objectives:

(i) The Global Caliphate
(ii) War with the West
(iii) Moral obligations of 'Jihad' and 'Hijra'
(iii) Religious legitimacy of Islam for the World
(iv) The Apocalypse of Islamic rule as God's Rule

The IS propagandits have been carrying out their agenda of extinction of Christianity and its long history and culture from Iraq, Syria, etc. They also compare and justify their 'missions' of 'jihad' in juxtaposition with the world-wide Christian missions and the old 'crusades' for the sake of the Kingdom of God. This has created an alarming rate of 'exodus' and 'migration' to the European countries.

The US-role for the creation of such a situation and their venomous 'silence' is not yet addressed by the world. Is it part of the US strategy to destabilize the European economy?

Islamic expansion in the West, especially in some of the European nations that have reached zero or minus growth-rate in populations is also another factor of concern. It is now almost sure that Islam will emerge as the 'first' among world's living religions for numerical strength and 'practicing'-record.

The comparatively 'peaceful' campaign of "Love-Jihad" or "Romeo-Jihad" is also not without its impact. The luring with love and marriage extended to women of other religions has also proved to some extent successful, as it is backed by 'money' power and other securities.

### (b) 'Hindutva' in India and the 'Ghar-Wapasi' slogan

Although the forces of 'Hindutva' are not so aggressive as comparable to the 'IS' and the extremist Islamic-forces, the 'secular' character of India is increasingly threatened by the new phases of hindutva-nationalism and hindutva-politics in alliance with its hidden 'economic' interests. Some of the liberal spokespersons of 'hindutva' would present 'hindutva' as a life-style and cultural ethos of India based on the principle of unity in diversity. But the growing tendency of setting certain 'criteria' for even legitimate diversities, is taking new turns.

In spite of the many militant threats and fundamentalist challenges of the modern Indian context, India still remains constitutionally safe for the practice and propagation of the Faiths of its citizens. But, it is time for more clarification on the "criteria" for 'hindutva sanskriti' and relevance of minority rights.

## 9. Concluding Suggestions on Fulfilling the Great Commission in our Context

(i) Mission in God's Way is an ongoing Mission. Jesus Christ's great Commission is invitation to participate in the same God's Mission (*Missio Dei*).

(ii) Disciples of Christ as individuals and communities are 'sent' to be authentic witnesses to and sharers of God's Mission.

(iii) Witnessing is in humility and self-emptying spirit with dimensions of 'mutual' **hospitality** in a spirit of **common pilgrimage** guided by the Holy Spirit towards all the truth.

(iv) Witnessing to God's Love manifested in Jesus Christ will lead to 'conversion'-experiences which nobody can stop.

(v) Making disciples to Jesus Christ, giving baptism and instructing to obey Jesus' commandments refer primarily to a qualitative change in conformity to the Way, the Truth and the Life, that is Jesus Christ.

(vi) While witnessing to and enjoying the salvation through Jesus Christ, we cannot set limits to the saving power of God and the universal salvific significance of the 'hidden' 'unknown' and 'unbound' Christ revealed in other religions. It also involves a courage to "risk" the 'bound' Christ of structures, social practices, rituals and doctrines that turn out to be barriers to the gospel.

(vii) The reality and growing awareness of multi-faith context must be taken as 'opportunity' not as 'threat' for authentic witnessing. Authentic witnessing implies ongoing conversion-experience even on the part of witnesses. It also implies cross-bearing 'confrontation'- struggles with the forces of fragmentation like casteism, communalism, sexism, religious fundamentalism, politicization of religion, 'ecomania' of 'Development', etc. This necessitates a human solidarity beyond the diverse identities of faiths and ideologies.

*Chapter 6*

# FULFILLING THE GREAT COMMISSION IN THE EMERGING MEDIA CONTEXT

Sham P. Thomas[1]

## 1. Introduction

I, basically, have structured this conversation under two basic headings: 'Observations about Mission' and that of 'Mission and Media' in order to make a few proposition for the church. For our understanding of mission, I have selected a biblical text (Luke 10:1-12) which is not the prescribed great commission text (Matthew 28:16-20).

Four observations can be made on this Lukan narrative on mission which, in turn, may provide a framework for understanding and accounting for our media practice even though the details of this connectivity is not exhaustively described.

### 1.1 Mission as moving to the third space

The suggestion of Mission as moving to the third space as the first observation on mission is to problematise the 'centre and the margin/periphery' discourse. Many a time the concept of '*Missio Dei*' envisages a movement from the centre to the

1 Rev Dr Sham P Thomas is Vicar of Mar Thoma Syrian Church Bangalore, Primrose Road. This presentation of Dr. Sham P. Thomas during the UTC Alumni Refresher Programme is documented by Rev. Anilal M. Jose and published here after being refined by the presenter.

margin. Those who disagree with such a concept, counter it with an alternative suggestion of mission being a movement in the opposite direction, i.e., from the margin to the centre.

I want to support the observation that Jesus transcended both the centre and periphery dichotomy in His time. Roman colonialism and Jewish synagogue rule constituted the 'centre' in Jesus' time where urban elite and hierarchical males reigned over everything. The poor, diseased and the peasant community were perceived as the 'margins'; who were called as the lost sheep. In such a centre-margin dichotomy or binary opposition, Jesus is being increasingly understood as having taken neither a pro-colonial nor a pro-margin approach. Of course, we tend to think that Jesus was pro-margin and many contextual theologies like liberation theology emphasised Jesus' identification with the poor and His preferential option for the poor. Even though this had brought in a new direction in our imagination and identification favouring the poor and the various marginalised sections, there is a need to problematize such a conceptualisation of favouring the margin as against the so called centre. Embracing either one of the binaries, that is, centre or the margin, will bring only, what is suggested as, 'repetition despite displacement.' If and when attempts are made to make the margin as the centre, then, invariably the so called centre will become the margin. If you start of from the supposed centre, and move to the margin, again the centre-margin dichotomy will remain. If the dichotomy persists irrespective of the starting point the result is the same. It is because of this conceptual confusion that *Basileia*, the kingdom of God, is perceived today as a third space, i.e., as an 'in-between interstitial space.' It is an in- between interstitial space, rather than an either- or space. In such conceptualisation, the third space accommodates and contests, abrogates and alters, the discourse of the centre and the margin, almost simultaneously.

In this vein, our understanding of mission as a move towards the third space will challenge and also include both the centre and the margin. It will neither romanticise either the centre nor the margin, but will be in a flux, in an interstitial moment moving towards neither to the centre nor to the margins, but to a third space. Even though, it is a conceptual perception, it is an invitation to move beyond the dichotomy and binary opposition reinforced by the centre and periphery discourse.

Let us examine, how the Kingdom of God, that is, *Basileia*, which Jesus came to inaugurate, signals a move towards a third space. Luke 10 narrates how in the sending of the evangelists/the unnamed people, Jesus was both mimicking and mocking the then existing practices. There were two practices with regard to sending: the Roman practice and the Jewish practice. In the Roman practice, send was a common word for despatching messengers or envoys in diplomatic settings. Moreover, Greco-Roman envoys were sent out frequently in pairs. The Jewish religion also practiced sending and that too in pairs.

Moses appointed seventy members as rulers and they moved away from an authoritarian power centering into shared authority. Genesis 10 mentions seventy nations being in the world even though the Greek version had it as seventy two. It is interesting to note that the same use of seventy and seventy two appears in Luke 10 as well depending on the different versions. Whether it is seventy or seventy two, the indication is towards universal mission. Jesus sends envoys for a new reign, a space which is universal. The chosen ones, however, do not represent hereditary, hierarchical, and patriarchal patterns of the centre. So also, even though they were authorised with power and authority, it was with vulnerability, which was not part of the power exhibition of the Jewish religious and Roman political centre. We know, in all cultures when a king send an envoy, whether it is a person or is it an animal, anyone who obstructs the same will be construed as challenging the authority of the king. As a result, the envoy will not be considered as vulnerable, but only as a symbol of Sender/King's might. In contrast to this, Jesus sent His envoys with power and vulnerability.

By sending seventy/seventy two people in mission Jesus was, in a way, mimicking both the Roman and Jewish sending and at the same time mocking, by bringing in an alteration. In other words, Jesus imitates and alters and thereby initiates a move to the third space. This is what I want to place before you as the first observation. Mission as moving to a third space, is a call to move beyond the centre – periphery binary. This will hold true for our discussion on Media as well.

## 1.2 Mission as Moving Together

The second observation on mission, based on the Lukan narrative, is that mission is a collaborative effort; not a competitive one. I take this queue from Jesus' practice of sending the evangelists/missionaries in pairs. It is not for an individual, solitary or competitive journey that Jesus had asked people to go. They were sent in pairs so as to indicate their mission as a collaborative and complementary task.

But, one cannot resist noticing that there is an intense competition among mission agencies today, even when it is not displayed publicly. So, the questions arise now are; in mission, where is this collaboration? Who is standing with whom? Where are we being together? Most of the time, the partakers in mission tend to assume the role of competitors rather than collaborators. This is an issue, at the practical level, we as pastors and church leaders have to address. Even within churches, there may be various organisations for mission which may end up perceiving one another as competitors. Even when they do not compete, do they co-operate or co-ordinate their activities? The very notion of being together in mission is increasingly becoming problematic. This raises various questions: being together in what? Is it in purpose? Is it in process? Is it by people? Or, is it only an idealised vision that we are holding on to? Other related questions are: do we learn from each other? Who correspond with each other? In this sense, what is the mission that is happening among those who are involved in mission? Are they only providers of mission rather than being receivers as well. How far, such a direction in the present day mission goes along with Jesus' practice of Mission as moving together in decision making, sharing the pain and joy?

## 1.3 Mission of the Anonymous

The third observation on mission, I want to submit is, about the anonymity of the mission agents in the Lukan narrative. Unlike the named apostles, Luke does not give the names of the seventy/seventy two missionaries. As it was with them, it is through the efforts and life of countless nameless persons that the reign of God has been witnessed or communicated to various places. One does not do mission work to earn a name or make a profit. But sadly, many mission organisations tend to become concerned more about fame and profit making, rather than participating in the mission. Some of their efforts in fund raising raise the question, whether there was an effort to project exaggerated results to convince the donors to pay money for the mission. The mission of the anonymous witnesses should serve as a counter to such tendencies. Moreover, we should also be aware that most of us are adherents of this religion and tradition because of the witness of our forefathers and foremothers who need not have been known or popular for their mission activities. While not discrediting the famed preachers or missionaries, we need to acknowledge and emulate those silent witnesses and their efforts to communicate the gospel in their generation and to their future generations. This is indeed a challenge in a culture of performance and marketing even in mission activities.

In addition to the anonymity of the mission agents, Luke also suggests, their lack of infrastructure support for mission. Jesus sent them without purse, bag and sandals. I want to assume from this biblical narrative, that for Jesus, it was not only the message of the missionaries but their mode of communication was also important. The infrastructure for mission- the way mission is done with- will communicate a message. In other words, It is not only what we preach from the pulpit, but the shape of the building in which we stand itself will communicate a message. This raises various challenges today. For instance, what do the elite language, high-tech evangelism, the latest model four wheeler and the most modern mission buildings convey? Our mission houses being the largest houses in many mission fields do convey a message! Will such houses symbolise the identification with the poor or the affluence of the mission agency? Jesus sent the disciples without the basic protection and sustenance to do the mission. Is it practical today?

## 1.4 Mission as of the Guest

The fourth observation regarding mission is, 'Mission as of the guest'. Mission is increasingly being perceived as hospitality, that is, we being the hosts. While not discrediting this notion, I want to reverse it to say that the mission is that of the guest. As per the Lukan narrative in discussion, missionaries were sent to be guests not hosts. They were sent as vulnerable guests whose stay and work depended on the type of reception they received. In this sense, they were not sent to be like guerrillas or army but as recipients of hospitality.

Disciples/Apostles/Missionaries being guest is not exclusive to this Lukan narrative alone. I may suggest that this is common to all mission narratives in the bible. Importantly, Jesus was a guest in many houses. Even after the resurrection, He was received as a guest by the two disciples at Emmaus. The imagery of Jesus knocking at the door in Revelation 3:20 is poignant, to say the least. Mission of Jesus, in this sense, depends on the response of the other and on the basis of establishing a relationship with the other. Missionary is the vulnerable person, whose mission depends on the reception he/she receives from the host.

The missionary as a guest indicates the receptivity to be exercised in mission. They are to accept the culture, tradition and custom of the receiving host without prejudice and condemnation. Luke suggests that "they were to eat what was served before them." What are the signs of our churches becoming the recipient of various cultures in India is a crucial question today? This is, however, not to romanticise the host and his/her culture. If mission agents are only to reaffirm the statusquo, there is no particular need for them to be there. On the other hand, mission agents cannot behave as if there is no goodness in a particular context either. In other words, while being a guest, the missionary is not expected to be a gullible one. Jesus went as a guest to many houses but did not refrain from challenging the hosts.

So far, we have been looking at the Lukan framework for mission. Mission is neither affirming the centre nor the margin; nor entering into a competitive spirit of conquering like army and engaging in a crusade; not showing institutional and money power in doing mission; but, to be a guest, but not as a gullible guest. How can we use this framework to understand communication in mission? This is what I want to address in the next part of this presentation.

In the media context, the church needs to be a guest. My proposition is: we need to move to a third space by moving away from the selective exclusion of media to its critical and creative use for communicating the gospel. The media history of the churches, so far, shows selective exclusion or selective embrace of media. It is from here that we need to move.

## 2. Media Practice of the Church in Mission: Exclusion and Embrace

I am not dealing with all the media in detail or separately. I take it for granted that you are aware of various media. But, let us look at how mainline churches have approached and used various media. I want to suggest that the church was selective and ambivalent in its relationship with various media.

## 2.1 Exclusion of Traditional Media and Performing Arts

When we examine the media history of the church, it becomes clear that folk songs, fine arts, and performance media like dance and drama were excluded by the Protestant, Mar Thoma and other mainline churches. There were exceptions but they were mostly confined to certain rural settings or to the 'margins'. Unsurprisingly, even when folk songs were used, they were not rated on par with hymns or lyrics.

When music and musical instruments are considered, it seems that casteism and purity-pollution notion had come into play in their acceptance or rejection. For instance, the string instruments were predominantly used by people of the so-called upper castes, while wind instruments were used by those of the so-called lower castes. The use of percussion instruments was also associated with the latter group. The wind instruments were considered as polluting, because of the possibility of saliva in them from its other users. The rejection of percussion instruments by the 'high castes' came from its use of the cow hides. On the contrary, such instruments were used with no such inhibitions by the 'lower' castes. Since, churches in India do have casteism in varying degrees; the use of different musical instruments within a particular church tradition itself would have been on caste lines. This may have been same case in the mission contexts too.

If folksongs and musical instruments had found its way into the church in some way, the entry of performance media like dance and drama, and fine arts were not possible at all. There seems to have even a phobia about the use of these media by the church. Apart from caste prejudices, there may have been four reasons why traditional and performing arts were excluded by the church.

(a) **Content:** The folk media content was not conducive to communicate Christian messages as it were mostly about local themes or folk myths.

(b) **Context and access:** The folk media or performance media were played in temples or the courtyards of feudal lords who were from the so-called high castes. People of other religions and caste groups were not given access even to watch these media lest participate in them. The lack of access led to lack of ability to use such media.

(c) **Condemnation by missionaries:** Western missionaries demonized certain media and media forms and dissuaded the christian converts from using them.

(d) **Condemnation of visual pleasure:** The puritanism that crept into *bhakti* tradition and also in mission discourse portrayed visual pleasure as sinful. Condemnation of visual pleasure may have brought in negativity towards dance, drama and visual media.

Such perceptions and practices may have been changing in the last few decades, but for many Christians, traditional media and performance arts continue to be less known, less used and less valued media. Even when it is used in mission communication, it is yet to be used significantly in the mainstream communication within the church.

## 2.2 Embrace of Print and Radio

Contrary to the traditional and performance media, church, mission agencies and missionaries did a somersault in embracing the Print and Radio media.

Churches, from the advent of the print medium, had shown an almost obsession for the medium aided by the printing of the Bible in various translations. There is still a prevalent notion among the churches that truth must be in print and anything that is not printed is not good. Literary and print medium had gained a hierarchically superior status among the churches. David Morgan had wonderfully catalogued how Protestants have produced pictures, even though they were against visual pleasures, and used them in tracts; and how print media came in as a large and important tool of mission. Radio also enjoyed a positive approach from the churches even though they were not using the medium as extensively as the print medium. One may remember the Christian broadcast from Srilanka radio during the second half of the twentieth century.

## 2.3 Exclusion of Films and Embrace of Television and Cyber Medium

Historically, the churches which embraced print and radio turned her back to film and cinema. Cinema and film-going were considered even as orgy, sinful and immoral. In my native place, about fifty years ago, when marriage alliances were proposed, one of the enquiries about the prospective groom was about his film viewing behaviour. If he was a film-goer, he would not have been considered as desirable by many christian families.

One of my professors had gone for preaching in a Tamil village a few decades ago. After his preaching, he went for a film in the night. The next evening he was not allowed to preach by people who happened to see him at the cinema the previous night! In short, film was not considered as anything good by the faithful. Of course, a few mission agencies use film in gospel communication but even now the mainline churches and their mission agencies do exhibit a hesitation about the film.

The ambivalence of the churches towards media comes into the fore again when we observe that the mission agencies or churches which excluded a visual medium like film were enthusiastic in embracing television and to watch films on television. My research had shown that there were at least four reasons why those who said 'no' to cinema had said 'yes' to television.

(a) **The viewing context:** Films were viewed in a dark hall where one does not know who all would be seated and it was a threatening context for many. On the contrary, television was viewed in the comfort of the home.

(b) **The confidence about audience composition and that of the content:** Cinema hall proposed an invariable mixing with an unknown group of various caste and class combination. As Television is a domestic medium, the audiences are known to one another and there is an undeclared confidence that the content would be of reasonable standard for a family audience. In other words, parents were comfortable to sit up with children to watch television, knowing that there won't be any sexual or related scenes popping upon the scene. Films would not offer any such comfort.

(c) **The control on the medium:** Having gone to a cinema after spending time on travel and money on ticket, one can only walkout in the event of not liking what is portrayed on the scenes. Television, on the other hand, offers more control on the medium with the possibility of switching off the set or changing channels without any cost or effort.

(d) **The tag of modernity:** Television came about as a gadget of modernity, like the radio and tape-recorder set. I am reminded of a few scenes from my childhood. About thirty or forty years ago it was an event to witness the arrival of our people from the Middle East on holidays. A large number of relatives would flock at the airport and would accord them a great welcome. The immigrant worker would invariably sport a sunglass, most probably of 'Ray ban' brand, and will have a big two in one (Radio cum Tape Recorder) set among his luggage! In the last two decades, especially in the Kerala context, things began to change. The number of relatives going to the airport may have changed, the taxi's hired for the purpose has given way for private vehicles and the Gulf returnee have stopped bringing the two in one set. Instead, they started bringing in a much larger luggage of a colour television set! In short, for many middle class families, television was not only an audio visual medium but also a gadget of modernity, progress and status!

If caste dispensation played a role in the reception/rejection of musical instruments, class affiliation played at least a small role in the acceptance of television medium. As churches and mission agencies were beneficiaries of modernity, they did not experience much discomfort in accepting this medium.

The embrace of television, however, signaled a major shift in the cultural practices and consumption of the protestant and reformed churches considering their apprehensions about visuals and images, especially, in religious affairs! This is the major media shift happened in the last ten years.

Again, those Protestants and other mainline church members, who abhor images and icons in the church buildings, have started marking their domestic spaces with numerous religious images, paintings and pictures! How do we explain this ambivalence between bare church walls and image-filled domestic religious space of the modern chrisitans?

When it comes to cyberspace, we see a hesitant but tolerant approach. It is, even today, the extreme fundamentalists, either on the right or on the left, are making use of the internet, for religious purposes and propaganda. The mainline churches and mission agencies have not condemned computer and internet, but are yet to engage them in a significant way.

The overview of the media practices of the churches suggests a selective embrace and exclusion. It is my submission that the churches and her mission have to move on from this ambivalence to a third space of critical embrace of all media. Let me explain, why it should be so?

## 3. Church and Communication

Church is the result of God's communication and church is created to continue God's communication. This communication should happen by employing all the available media at any given point in time. Because,

(a) **Incarnation is entering into the frame of reference of the audience:** We need to meet people where they are. So also, we need to pitch our tent where they are, so that we may enter into their frame of reference. This the incarnational principle embodied in Jesus and hence our theological foundation for embracing mission in the mediascape.

(b) **Media space itself has become a mission field:** Media is no longer a neutral tool for communication. Media constitute a field of its own and hence it should be considered as a mission field. There is a mission in this field; there is a mission through this field; there is a mission about this field. Mission is not only to institutions and structures; mission is not only to peoples and countries; mission should be to the mediascape itself.

(c) **Media create a new religious public space:** We want mission communication in the public space. Earlier understanding of the public space was about a geographic space where people used to congregate. This was essential for the agricultural and industrial societies. The information society, in which we live today, provides an additional space for people to get connected, and that is the mediascape. In the present time, media has become the prominent public space. Church and mission agencies can avoid this space only at its peril.

Again, such engagement with the media is not to romanticise them but to affirm its goodness and also to offer a critique on it. It is in this sense that we can offer a prophetic solidarity to the media.

Let me conclude with a quote from Pope John Paul II: "For the Church the new world of mediascape is a summons to the great adventure of using its potential to proclaim the Gospel message. This challenge is ...to follow the Lord's command to 'put out into the deep': Duc in altum! (Luke 5:4)."

It is my wish and prayer that we move into the deep. We are not to move as guerrillas or army; but as guests, as vulnerable people, making use of the various options available in the media space, by being present there, not as gullible guests, but as prophets who offers critical solidarity, so that the churches will move together with God- who will be present wherever two or three people meet, either in a room or on the net, in His name- to the third space of *Basileia*.

*Chapter 7*

# BEING TOGETHER
## FLOURISHING OF CREATION

**Siddhartha**[1]

### 1. Introduction

The notion of environment was not part of our vocabulary in my student days. Development was seen as positive provided there was equity. We now find ourselves in a somewhat confused period where some are even stating that growth oriented development is at the root of our climate woes. A few have proposed that we get rid of the notion of development altogether and look at sustainable futures within a paradigm of zero growth. It is not always clear what this really means and how to bring about the necessary changes without rocking the boat perilously. Many argue that such alternatives are utopian and that the best we can hope for is to reform within the existing system, although that is clearly not enough to prevent the impending catastrophe.

Nothing had prepared us for the advent of the climate crisis. In a study completed in 2013, Professor Steven Sherwood from the University of New South Wales in Australia said that the planet would see an increase in temperature

---

1 Mr. Siddhartha is the Founder of the Fireflies Ashram & Intercultural Centre Dinnepalya, Bangalore. This presentation of Mr. Siddhartha during the UTC Alumni Refresher Programme is documented by Mr. Aby K. Thomas and is published here after being refined by the presenter.

of 4°C by 2100 if greenhouse emissions were not reduced.[2] This is twice the level regarded as dangerous by climate scientists.

## 2. Climate Change Implications for the Indian Coastal Ecosystem

Unfortunately, sufficient studies to determine projections on climate change impact on fish populations in India's coastal waters have not been done so far. But figures show that the annual per capita fish catch by artisanal fishers in the country dropped from 2,590 kg in 1980 to 420 kg in 1996-97. This is due to a combination of climate factors, chemical pollution of the sea waters and fishing with mechanized boats and trawlers. The livelihood of small fisherfolk has been badly affected as fish stocks dwindle. For example, the state of Maharashtra's annual fish catch has declined from 4.5 lakh tones in 2002 to 2.25 lakh tones in 2010[3], and artisanal fish workers are the most seriously affected by this.

Fish populations in the coastal waters are facing the usual problems of overfishing, pollution (garbage, including plastic waste, chemical waste) and habitat degradation. Catching of juvenile fish reduce the fish population substantially. Fish stocks are also affected by changes in species composition of phytoplankton at higher temperatures.[4] Marine phytoplanktons are tiny plants that represent food for fish and suck up carbon dioxide and release oxygen. They are declining rapidly as a result of a loss of nutrients with the warming of seas. Worldwide phytoplankton levels have gone down by 40% since the 1940s. Apart from this the oceans also absorb about 26% of carbon dioxide emerging from a variety of human activities. This process happens with the help of different marine living organisms and habitats that include mangroves, salt marshes, sea grasses and seaweed, frequently referred to as 'blue forests'.

Rising acidity levels in the seas as a result of climate change have harmful effects on coral reefs and calcium-bearing organisms.[5] Coral reefs support about one million species. In the Indian seas, coral reefs are found in the Gulf of Mannar, Gulf of Kutch, Palk Bay, Andaman Sea and Lakshadweep Sea. Rising carbon dioxide concentration is leading to acidification of the sea damaging these coral reefs. Coral bleaching is already happening in a noticeable way in the Andaman

---

2 Steven C. Sherwood, et al., "Spread in model climate sensitivity traced to atmospheric convective mixing", Nature 505 (02 January 2014), 37–42 (accessed on June 4, 2015), doi:10.1038/nature12829.

3 Prabhakar Nair, "The Coastal Eco Region – Vulnerabilities of Fishing Communities to Ecological and Climate Change", in *Voices of Vulnerability-Choices of Change*, ed. John D'Souza (INECC, 2012), 53.

4 E. Vivekanandan , "Impact and Adaptation Options for Indian Marine Fisheries to Climate Change", 65, Madras Research Centre of Central Marine Fisheries Research Institute, Chennai 600 028, (accessed on June 5, 2015, http://eprints.cmfri.org.in/9832/1/ICT_Oriented_Strategic_Extension_for_Responsible_Fisheries_Management_Manual-87-96.pdf.

5 Ibid.

Sea. It is believed that coral reefs will disappear in about 50 years' time. About 25% of the world's marine species are today found in coral reefs.

Saline water entering coastal farms is negatively affecting the agricultural production of small farmers in coastal areas in India. The situation has become untenable in places like the Sunderban Islands. Salt water is also intruding into the drinking water of villagers along the coast. Reports from Kerala indicate that the sea is slowly battering about 200 fishing villages. According to the Kerala Swathanthra Matsya Thozhilali Federation (Kerala Independent Fish Workers Federation) about 10,000 people will be rendered homeless along the Kerala-Kanyakumari coast.[6] As far as beach erosion is concerned, India was ranked as the most vulnerable of the 51 countries by IPCC (Intergovernmental Panel on Climate Change) scientists.[7] The experience of the Maharashtra coast shows that warmer seas might lead to more cyclones and storm surges.[8] Bangladesh and India account for 86% of the mortality from tropical cyclones and severe storms.[9]

## 3. Forest Communities and Climate Change

As a result of the pressures of development and global warming forest eco-systems in India will undergo changes in species composition, productivity and bio-diversity. Like other parts of the world forest communities and forests in India face major challenges from mining, timber and land mafia as well as the construction of factories, roads and railway lines. In 1974, the well-known Chipko movement had peasant women from Himalayan villages in Uttarakhand hugging trees to prevent them being felled by the contractors. In many parts of India forest communities depend on rain-fed agriculture. They also collect Non-Timber Forest Products (NTFP) also known as Minor Forest Products (MFP), that include honey, medicinal and aromatic plants (MAP), oil seeds, fiber & floss, resins, edible plants, bamboo, reeds and grasses. Unfortunately, the forest communities continue to face difficulties due to the government's tardiness in implementing the Forest Rights Act, which gives them ownership rights of land

---

6 Prabhakar Nair, "Vulnerabilities of Fishing Communities to Ecological and Climate Change" in Voices of Vulnerability-Choices of Change, ed. John D'Souza (INECC, 2012), 56 (accessed on June 6, 2015), http://ced.org.in/docs/inecc/Voices_of_Vulnerability/VV-Coastal-eco-region.pdf.

7 Anupam Chakravartty, "Expect more extreme climate events in India", Down to Earth (31 March 2014), (accessed on June 6, 2015), http://www.downtoearth.org.in/content/expect-more-extreme-climate-events-india.

8 Prabhakar Nair, "Vulnerabilities of Fishing Communities to Ecological and Climate Change" in Voices of Vulnerability-Choices of Change, ed. John D'Souza (INECC, 2012), 72 (accessed on June 6, 2015), http://ced.org.in/docs/inecc/Voices_of_Vulnerability/VV-Coastal-eco-region.pdf.

9 Anupam Chakravartty, "Expect more extreme climate events in India", Down to Earth (31 March 2014), (accessed on June 6, 2015), http://www.downtoearth.org.in/content/expect-more-extreme-climate-events-india.

they have traditionally possessed along with the rights to livelihood. Climate change is definitely staring at them in the face as it reduces bio-diversity and threatens food security.

The Adivasi (tribal) populations of the state of Odisha have been struggling to prevent their lands being taken over for mining and industrial purposes. Two giant projects of multinational corporations have been hanging fire as a result of the Adivasi struggles. The South Korean company POSCO faced long delays in setting up their its massive steel plant on Adivasi lands. Unfortunately the government of India has given the green signal for this plant to take off. As for the Vedanta bauxite mine at Niyamgiri the Adivasi struggles appear to have produced results. In January 2014, the central government rejected Vedanta's proposal to clear the forests to start bauxite mining. The state government of Odisha has now appealed to the Supreme Court challenging this decision. The recognition of indigenous peoples' rights over their forests and the significance of their role in forest management are of crucial importance in dealing with climate change impacts.

Forests in the earth's carbon cycle play a significant role. Trees cannot absorb carbon when forests are cut down. When wood is burned or decays the carbon absorbed by trees is released as carbon dioxide. While croplands also store carbon, forests store between 20 and 100 times more carbon per unit area.[10] In the context of climate change the United Nations is attempting to help developing countries protect, better manage and save forest resources through a program called REDD (Reducing Emissions from Deforestation and Forest Degradation). REDD Plus is not only concerned with checking deforestation and forest degradation but also includes positive efforts at conservation, sustainable management and enhancement of forest carbon stocks. The Forest Rights Act in India is meant to empower forest communities to participate in the use and management of forest resources. However civil society groups are wary of the government and suspect that the government will use REDD Plus to weaken the Forest Rights Act.[11]

## 4. The Urban Context and Climate Change

India's urban population is likely to grow to 875 million people by 2050, representing 54 per cent of the total population.[12] This is more than the

10 "Forests and Climate Change" in Forests Forever (accessed on June 6, 2015), http://www.forestsforever.org/climate2.html.

11 Ashish Aggarwal, "Implementation of Forest Rights Act, Changing Forest Landscape, and 'Politics of REDD+' in India" in Resources, Energy, and Development 8(2) (New Delhi: Teri, September 2011), 131–148 (accessed on June 6, 2015), http://www.teriin.org/projects/nfa/cc2bwp2.php.

12 "By 2050, 54% of India population to shift to urbanised cities", Modified on 7 April 2012, Commodity Online, (accessed on June 6, 2015), http://www.commodityonline.com/news/by-2050-54-of-india-population-to-shift-to-urbanised-cities-47263-3-47264.html.

current combined population of USA, Brazil, Russia, Japan and Germany. In Mumbai, India's second largest city, about nine million people, or 62% of the city's population, live in slums.[13] By 2017, India's slum population is slated to rise to 104 million people.[14] In many of the slums there is little sanitation or electricity and inadequate water supply. Often slums are located in low-lying areas that are prone to flooding. In coastal cities there is evidence of increased flooding in the past few years. Kolkatta city has been ranked as the seventh most perilous urban conglomeration as far as storms, storm surges, tsunamis and river floods are concerned.[15] In 2005, Mumbai was struck by a cyclone that brought 94 centimeters of rain in 24 hours. More than a thousand people died.[16] The government of Maharashtra developed India's first urban disaster management plan for the city of Mumbai but very little follow-up action was taken to implement it. Poor housing conditions, no adherence to building regulations and lack of land tenure increase the woes of people in the slums.

A city like Bengaluru was known as the garden city of India not too long ago. Today, many of the trees have been cut as part of the road-widening program and old houses were knocked down to build apartments. The massive increase in the number of cars, motorcycles, buses and trucks in the city have dramatically increased emissions. Air Pollution in some parts of the city is three to four times higher than the permissible limits![17] Municipal authorities have to come up with plans to deal with emissions that come from power usage, vehicle use and waste management (waste releases huge amounts of methane and other gases). Waste is also taken from the cities and dumped in nearby villages, creating health hazards to the local people.

---

13 Bhavika Jain, "62% of Mumbai lives in slums: Census", Updated on October 17, 2010, Hindustan Times (accessed on June 6, 2015), http://www.hindustantimes.com/india-news/mumbai/62-of-mumbai-lives-in-slums-census/article1-614027.aspx.

14 Dipak Kumar Dash, "By 2017, India's slum population will rise to 104 million", Updated on August 20, 2013, Times of India (accessed on June 6, 2015), http://timesofindia.indiatimes.com/india/By-2017-Indias-slum-population-will-rise-to-104-million/articleshow/21927474.cms.

15 Sayantan Bera, "Kolkata is one of world's 10 cities most at risk from natural disasters", Updated on March 27, 2014, Down to Earth (accessed on June 6, 2015), http://www.downtoearth.org.in/content/kolkata-one-world-s-10-cities-most-risk-natural-disasters.

16 Architesh Panda, "Climate Change Risks & Adaptation: Indian Mega Cities", in The India Economy Review, January 1, 2011 (accessed on June 6, 2015), http://theindiaeconomyreview.org/Article.aspx?aid=30&mid=3.

17 Vinayashree Jagadeesh, "City's air dangerously polluted", The Hindu, August 25, 2014 (accessed on June 6, 2015), http://www.thehindu.com/todays-paper/citys-air-dangerously-polluted/article6348230.ece.

## 5. Climate Change and Mountainous Regions

Mountain systems represent about 20% of the earth's surface. According to an IPCC (Intergovernmental Panel on Climate Change) report "mountains provide the direct life-support base for about a tenth of humankind and indirectly affect the lives of more than half."[18] In India, mountainous regions provide water, electricity, biological diversity, minerals, forest, vegetables and other agricultural produce. There is evidence that temperatures in the Himalayas are rising faster than the global average. Surface air temperatures in the Himalayas have gone up by one degree in the last decade.[19] The Himalayan glaciers lost about 174 giga tons of water between 2003 and 2009, causing ruinous floods in the Indus, Ganges and Brahmaputra rivers. Pollution is also contributing to the melting of glaciers as an 'Asian brown cloud' comprising of 2 million particles of soot and dark particles enter the atmosphere every year due to pollution in India and China.[20]

Due to over exploitation many mountainous regions in India are losing their forest cover leading to frequent landslides. In addition there is loss of bio-diversity and loss of medicinal plants. In the past few decades tourism has become a major economic activity adding to the environment woes. In some mountain areas the increase in the number of people has led to over grazing of livestock and deforestation. In June 2013, flash floods in Uttarakhand led to the death of about 1000 people. Roads, bridges and other infrastructure were washed away and thousands of homes destroyed. If the region had not been so badly deforested the impact of the floods would have been less pronounced.[21]

## 6. Health and the Climate Crisis

The increase of droughts, diseases, floods, famine, extreme heat and humidity are partly the result of warming temperatures and variable precipitation. The direct and indirect results of rising temperatures are malnutrition, decrease in water availability, and spread of diseases like malaria, chikungunya, dengue and diarrheal illnesses. Dehydration, heat exhaustion and heat stroke are other health problems

---

18 Martin Beniston and Douglas G. Fox, "Impacts of climate change on Mountains" in Climate Change 2014: Impacts, Adaptation, and Vulnerability, IPCC AR5 (March 2014). 194 (accessed on June 6, 2015), https://ipcc-wg2.gov/AR5/images/uploads/WGIIAR5-PartA_FINAL.pdf.

19 Mukesh Ray et al., "Mountain Eco-region-Climate Vulnerability in North Western Himalayas" in Voices of Vulnerability-Choices of Change, ed. John D'Souza (INECC, 2012), 15 (accessed on June 6, 2015), http://ced.org.in/docs/inecc/Voices_of_Vulnerability/VV-mountain-eco-region.pdf.

20 Javaid Laghari, "Climate change: Melting glaciers bring energy uncertainty", Nature-International Weekly Journal of Science (15 November 2013) (accessed on June 6, 2015), http://www.nature.com/news/climate-change-melting-glaciers-bring-energy-uncertainty-1.14031.

21 "Uttarakhand Flash Flood-A Report", Indian Red Cross Society (June 27, 2013) (acccessed on June 6, 2015), http://www.indianredcross.org/press-rel27-june2013.htm.

that will affect a large number of people, mainly the poorer Indians. The elderly, young children and newborns are particularly at risk when temperatures rise. People's productivity also goes down with higher humidity and temperatures.

A study done by Srinath Reddy and Dileep Mavalankar in the city shows that construction and factory workers, manual labourers and women working in ill-ventilated kitchens are particularly vulnerable to heat stress. For people in the city the lakes, parks, trees and bus stations provide some respite from the heat.[22] The concentration of regional air pollutants and aeroallergens will increase with warmer temperatures. This will lead to an increase in respiratory disorders such as asthma, emphysema and chronic bronchitis, and allergy problems. As a result of vehicular pollution smog will also increase in the cities. Again this will lead to asthma and respiratory infections in children, chronic obstructive pulmonary disease and pneumothorax. Air pollution is also likely to increase the incidence of tuberculosis. Malaria, dengue and chikungunya are reportedly on the rise in different parts of South Asia. It is generally agreed that malaria will increase in places where temperatures exceed 40°C. Adaptation measures can be further improved by documenting and disseminating the practices of local communities who face floods, heat strokes and mosquito bites.[23]

## 7. Food and the Climate Crisis

There may be a ten percent decrease in food grain production for every one degree rise in temperature, if one goes by the thumb rule provided by Lester Brown in his book 'PLAN B'. For a country like India this means a thirty to forty percent reduction in food grain production by the end of the century depending on whether the temperature has gone up by three or four degrees Celsius. Decreasing food availability can also lead to significant health problems, including childhood stunting, which is projected to increase by 35% by 2050 compared to a scenario without climate change."[24] The report further states that if temperatures go up by 2°C-2.5°C compared to pre-industrial levels, it will impact food security for some 63 million people. This would be due to reduction in water for agricultural production in the river basins of the Indus, Ganges and Brahmaputra. Although the green revolution was seen as a spectacular success in India, putting behind the

22 Dileep Mavalankar, et al., "Climate Change and Health Preparedness in India: Protecting Local Communities in Ahmedabad, Gujarat from Extreme Heat", Natural Resources Defense Council (2012). 8 (accessed on June 6, 2015), http://www.nrdc.org/international/india/files/IndiaHealthReport.pdf.

23 Poonam K. Singh & Ramesh C. Dhiman, "Climate change and human health: Indian context", Journal of Vector Borne Diseases 49 (June 2012), 55–60 (accessed on June 6, 2015), http://www.mrcindia.org/journal/issues/492055.pdf.

24 "Warming Climate in India to Pose Significant Risk to Agriculture, Water Resources, Health" The World Bank Press Release (June 19, 2013), (accessed on June 6, 2015), http://www.worldbank.org/en/news/press-release/2013/06/19/warming-climate-india-pose-significant-risk-agriculture-water-resources-health-says-world-bank-report.

days of famine and mass hunger, only a few people commented on the lack of sustainable practices. Even fewer alerted us to the fact that it took place in places where irrigation was present, and that 60 per cent of the cultivated area in India is not irrigated but rainfed. Today, as we learn of the specter of food shortages in the decades ahead, induced by the climate crisis, there are calls for a second green revolution in rainfed areas; but this time a more sustainable one.

## 8. The Importance of Millets

While millets are well known in India many other parts of the world people are still ignorant of them; most have not even heard of the term. In south India, there is an old Kannada saying which extols the virtues of finger millets, known as ragi among the local people: "The rice eater is weightless like a bird; the one who eats jowar millet is strong like a wolf; and the one who eats ragi is 'nirogi' (illness free) throughout his life."

Culturally millets are still considered the food of the poor. The whiteness of rice unfortunately adds to its superiority. Rice is also given a higher status since it is the food of the upper castes while the poor lower castes eat millets. Today even the poor are slowly giving up millets for high status rice![25] Millets are among the oldest cereal grains to be used for domestic consumption in India. They are considered seeded grasses that grow well in dry zones even in poor soil with little moisture. The main millets cultivated in India are Finger millets (Ragi), Sorghum (known as Jowar in Karnataka), Pearl millet (Sajje), Foxtail millet (Navane), Little millet, Kodo millet, Proso millet and Barnyard millet. Millets provide superior nutrition compared to rice and wheat. In a nutritionally deficient country like India, millets are three to five times better than rice and wheat in providing proteins, minerals and vitamins.

Poor and degraded soil is not a hindrance to cultivate millets. Besides, the soil depth can be less than 15cm. Since millets are usually grown within a mixed farming approach, the soil is considerably enriched with additional rows of pulses (red gram, cowpea, beans, green gram, black gram, lentils) and oilseeds. Most millet farmers do not use synthetic fertilizers at all. A little farmyard manure will suffice. Therefore the government can save some money by reducing the use of subsidized synthetic fertilizers. Since millets are also pest resistant they do not require chemical pesticides. With agricultural emissions representing about 12% of total emissions growing millets can prove to be an effective climate mitigation strategy as well, since most millet farmers do not use chemical fertilizers and pesticides, which contribute to greenhouse gases. Avoiding chemical fertilizers and pesticides also reduces the pollution of ground water.

Growing millets is also a good adaptation strategy for poor farmers since they do not need irrigation. Millets are also much sturdier to withstand fluctuating

---

25 Rahmat Tarikere, "Food et cetera", 2010 (accessed on June 6, 2015), http://www.india-seminar.com/2010/612/612_rahmat_tarikere.htm.

rainfall and temperatures. Rice and wheat will take a beating in India as climate change kicks in. Millets have a greater capacity to sequester carbon dioxide as they have bigger leaves than rice or wheat. The bigger leaves and larger stalks contribute to increasing fodder stock for cattle. Government policies have also contributed to diminishing the importance of millets since the Public Distribution System (PDS) largely distributes only rice and wheat. This is a kind of Sanskritisation.[26] Sanskritisation is an expression coined by the Indian social anthropologist M.N.Srinivas to denote the manner in which lower castes imitated the higher castes in some matters to raise their social status. In this case the lower castes are imitating the higher castes in their preference for rice and wheat over millets

## 9. Conclusion

Albert Einstein said that no problem could be solved with the same nature of consciousness that created the problem in the first place.[27] We cannot hope to struggle against climate change with the same consciousness that was responsible for creating it in the first place. In the consciousness of some people the world is a commodity to be exploited for profit. They refer to the earth as real estate, resource, mineral and property. At the altar of money they are prepared to pollute and destroy the life enhancing potential of planet earth.

In traditional India, the value of the simple life was deeply ingrained in the cultural ethos. Human fulfillment was not measured in terms of one's wealth or possessions. The cult of consumerism was totally absent. People recognized the greatness of Gandhi because of his simple life. If he had lived differently he would not have been the mahatma or great soul, and India's non-violent freedom struggle might have taken a different turn. We are all inter-connected and we live in an interdependent planet. The pollution emanating from the USA, China and India will eventually drown a country like Bangladesh, whose ecological footprint is very low. All things are connected, for both good and bad. The story of Indra's net tells us this.

In the heavenly abode of the great god Indra hangs a marvelous and immense net. This vast net opens out in all directions. At each node of the net hangs a single sparkling jewel. Numerous jewels hang in this infinite net. Each jewel glitters away, sparkling like a star, suspended in the net. But if one looks closely one realizes that each jewel reflects all the other jewels in the net. The process of reflection is infinite. If each of us is a jewel in Indra's net then we are all connected with each other. Our dazzle and glitter largely comes from the reflection of the reflection of all the other jewels in the infinite net. We are all influenced and

---

26 "Supporting Millets in India: Policy Review and Suggestions for Action", Dhan Foundation (August 2012). 11 (accessed on June 6, 2015), http://www.dhan.org/smallmillets/docs/report/Millet_Support_Policies.pdf.

27 "Albert Einstein" (accessed on June 6, 2015), http://en.wikiquote.org/wiki/Talk:Albert_Einstein.

enhanced by each other. If one jewel ceases to sparkle every other jewel is affected. Likewise if one jewel glitters more brightly, every jewel glitters more brightly. Every compassionate act affects the whole web. So if we do something to protect life on the planet that action influences everybody else on the planet, even if we are not conscious of it. Each action helps to build up the critical mass, which, when reached, can bring the miraculous change we all dream about.

## Bibliography

Steven C. Sherwood, et al., "Spread in model climate sensitivity traced to atmospheric convective mixing", Nature 505 (02 January 2014): 37-42 (accessed on June 4, 2015), doi:10.1038/nature12829.

Prabhakar Nair, "The Coastal Eco Region – Vulnerabilities of Fishing Communities to Ecological and Climate Change", in *Voices of Vulnerability-Choices of Change*, ed. John D'Souza (INECC, 2012), 53.

E. Vivekanandan, "Impact and Adaptation Options for Indian Marine Fisheries to Climate Change.", Madras Research Centre of Central Marine Fisheries Research Institute. 65 (accessed on June 5, 2015), http://eprints.cmfri.org.in/9832/1/ICT_Oriented_Strategic_Extension_for_Responsible_Fisheries_Management_Manual-87-96.pdf.

E. Vivekanandan, "Impact and Adaptation Options for Indian Marine Fisheries to Climate Change.", Madras Research Centre of Central Marine Fisheries Research Institute. 63 (accessed on June 5, 2015), http://eprints.cmfri.org.in/9832/1/ICT_Oriented_Strategic_Extension_for_Responsible_Fisheries_Management_Manual-87-96.pdf.

Prabhakar Nair, "Vulnerabilities of Fishing Communities to Ecological and Climate Change" in Voices of Vulnerability-Choices of Change, ed. John D'Souza (INECC, 2012), 56 (accessed on June 6, 2015), http://ced.org.in/docs/inecc/Voices_of_Vulnerability/VV-Coastal-eco-region.pdf.

Anupam Chakravartty, "Expect more extreme climate events in India", Down to Earth (31 March 2014) (accessed on June 6, 2015), http://www.downtoearth.org.in/content/expect-more-extreme-climate-events-india.

Prabhakar Nair, "Vulnerabilities of Fishing Communities to Ecological and Climate Change" in Voices of Vulnerability-Choices of Change, ed. John D'Souza (INECC, 2012), 72 (accessed on June 6, 2015), http://ced.org.in/docs/inecc/Voices_of_Vulnerability/VV-Coastal-eco-region.pdf.

Anupam Chakravartty, "Expect more extreme climate events in India", Down to Earth (31 March 2014) (accessed on June 6, 2015), http://www.downtoearth.org.in/content/expect-more-extreme-climate-events-india.

"Forests and Climate Change" in Forests Forever (accessed on June 6, 2015), http://www.forestsforever.org/climate2.html.

Ashish Aggarwal, "Implementation of Forest Rights Act, changing forest landscape, and 'politics of REDD+' in India" in Resources, Energy, and Development 8(2) (New Delhi: Teri, September 2011), 131–148 (accessed on June 6, 2015), http://www.teriin.org/projects/nfa/cc2bwp2.php.

"By 2050, 54% of India population to shift to urbanised cities", Modified on 7 April 2012, Commodity Online (accessed on June 6, 2015), http://www.commodityonline.com/news/by-2050-54-of-india-population-to-shift-to-urbanised-cities-47263-3-47264.html.

Bhavika Jain, "62% of Mumbai lives in slums: Census", Updated on October 17, 2010, Hindustan Times. (accessed on June 6, 2015), http://www.hindustantimes.com/india-news/mumbai/62-of-mumbai-lives-in-slums-census/article1-614027.aspx.

Dipak Kumar Dash, "By 2017, India's slum population will rise to 104 million", Updated on August 20, 2013, Times of India (accessed on June 6, 2015), http://timesofindia.indiatimes.com/india/By-2017-Indias-slum-population-will-rise-to-104-million/articleshow/21927474.cms.

Sayantan Bera, "Kolkata is one of world's 10 cities most at risk from natural disasters", Updated on March 27, 2014, Down to Earth (accessed on June 6, 2015), http://www.downtoearth.org.in/content/kolkata-one-world-s-10-cities-most-risk-natural-disasters.

Architesh Panda, "Climate Change Risks & Adaptation: Indian Mega Cities", in The India Economy Review, January 1, 2011 (accessed on June 6, 2015), http://theindiaeconomyreview.org/Article.aspx?aid=30&mid=3.

Vinayashree Jagadeesh, "City's air dangerously polluted", The Hindu, August 25, 2014 (accessed on June 6, 2015), http://www.thehindu.com/todays-paper/citys-air-dangerously-polluted/article6348230.ece.

Martin Beniston and Douglas G. Fox, "Impacts of climate change on Mountains" in Climate Change 2014: Impacts, Adaptation, and Vulnerability, IPCC AR5 (March 2014). 194 (accessed on June 6, 2015), https://ipcc-wg2.gov/AR5/images/uploads/WGIIAR5-PartA_FINAL.pdf.

Mukesh Ray et al., "Mountain Eco-region-Climate Vulnerability in North Western Himalayas" in *Voices of Vulnerability-Choices of Change*, ed. John D'Souza (INECC, 2012), 15 (accessed on (June 6, 2015), http://ced.org.in/docs/inecc/Voices_of_Vulnerability/VV-mountain-eco-region.pdf.

Javaid Laghari, "Climate change: Melting glaciers bring energy uncertainty", Nature-International Weekly Journal of Science (15 November 2013), (accessed on June 6, 2015), http://www.nature.com/news/climate-change-melting-glaciers-bring-energy-uncertainty-1.14031.

"Uttarakhand Flash Flood-A Report", Indian Red Cross Society (June 27, 2013), (accessed on June 6, 2015), http://www.indianredcross.org/press-rel27-june2013.htm.

Dileep Mavalankar, et al., "Climate Change and Health Preparedness in India: Protecting Local Communities in Ahmedabad, Gujarat from Extreme Heat", Natural Resources Defense Council (2012). 8 (accessed on June 6, 2015), http://www.nrdc.org/international/india/files/IndiaHealthReport.pdf.

Poonam K. Singh & Ramesh C. Dhiman, "Climate change and human health: Indian context", Journal of Vector Borne Diseases 49 (June 2012), 55–60 (accessed on June 6, 2015), http://www.mrcindia.org/journal/issues/492055.pdf.

"Warming Climate in India to Pose Significant Risk to Agriculture, Water Resources, Health" The World Bank Press Release (June 19, 2013) (accessed on June 6, 2015), http://www.worldbank.org/en/news/press-release/2013/06/19/warming-climate-india-pose-significant-risk-agriculture-water-resources-health-says-world-bank-report.

Rahmat Tarikere, "Food et cetera", 2010 (accessed on June 6, 2015), http://www.india-seminar.com/2010/612/612_rahmat_tarikere.htm.

"Supporting Millets in India: Policy Review and Suggestions for Action", Dhan Foundation (August 2012). 11 (accessed on June 6, 2015) , http://www.dhan.org/smallmillets/docs/report/Millet_Support_Policies.pdf.

"Albert Einstein" (accessed on June 6, 2015), http://en.wikiquote.org/wiki/Talk:Albert_Einstein.

*Chapter 8*

# BEING TOGETHER
## HEALTH AND WHOLENESS

**Arul Dhas T**[1]

I am grateful to the United Theological College, my Alma Mater and the organisers of the Refresher course this year for this opportunity to bring some of my random thoughts from my 26 year old ministry in the Christian Medical College, Vellore. I thank God for the convenor Dr. Santhosh Kumar for his gentle words, approach and attitude.

In this presentation, I would like to share with you three important things. First of all, how does the ministry of healing fits in the great commission of our Lord Jesus Christ. Secondly, what do I understand by this phrase 'being together' in the context of our calling and ministry. Finally, I would highlight some methods and approaches the healthcare institutions adopt to achieve the purpose of 'being together'.

### 1. Great Commission of our Lord Jesus Christ

"Go therefore and make disciples of all nations, baptizing them in the name of the Father and of the Son and of the Holy Spirit, and teaching them to obey everything that I have commanded you." Matthew 28:19, 20 is often referred to as the great commission. However, we see that many ignore the Johannine version of the great commission: "As the Father has sent me, so I send you" "Receive the

1 Rev. Dr. Arul Dhas T. is a Senior Chaplain at the Christian Medical College, Vellore.

Holy Spirit. If you forgive the sins of any, they are forgiven them; if you retain the sins of any, they are retained" (John 20: 21).

Whether in the rendering of Matthew or John, the ministry of healing and wholeness – a ministry of salvation is envisaged. How does the whole creation receive and experience the 'fulness of life' seems to be the focus through the great commission. When some of us who experienced the new life, it becomes our mandate to share and communicate this new life with others.

## 2. Being Together

Health was understood by Hippocrates (c 460-377 BCE) as "a delicate balance of four fluids: blood, yellow bile, black bile, and phlegm."[2] The World Health Organisation has been defining health as "a complete state of physical, mental and social well-being, and not merely the absence of disease or infirmity."[3] Australian Aboriginal people generally define health not just the physical well-being of the individual but "the social, emotional, spiritual and cultural well-being of the whole community."[4]

God is one. In this oneness is wholeness. Even though we are different parts, as long as we are together we can experience that oneness. 'Estrangement' is sin. When we are not together, we experience brokenness. Being together is about oneness.

Some components of Healing ministry:

For Jesus, the healing ministry was an expression of Kingdom characteristics. God is the healer therefore through the healing events, Jesus proclaimed the nature of God. The healing events are declared as miracles or signs in the gospel writings.

Through the history, the body of Christ, the church has taken this part of the ministry as one of the threefold ministries (Preaching, Teaching and Healing). In the places like India, structurally, this is portrayed by the building of a Church, School and Dispensary/Hospital.

Major part of my working life has been in a hospital. Therefore, my reflections and thinking are shaped by the life experiences in a hospital. In this presentation, I would like to highlight some processes and events which I think have been helpful to bring forth health and wholeness.

---

2 Üstün & Jakob. "Redefining 'Health'", Bulletin of the World Health Organization, 2005; 83:802, http://www.who.int/bulletin/bulletin_board/83/ustun11051/en/

3 WHO. Preamble to the Constitution of the World Health Organization as adopted by the International Health Conference, New York, 19-22 June 1946, and entered into force on 7 April 1948, http://www.who.int/about/definition/en/print.html.

4 National Health and Medical Research Council. Promoting the health of Indigenous Australians. A review of infrastructure support for Aboriginal and Torres Strait Islander health advancement. Final report and recommendations. Canberra: NHMRC, 1996: part 2: 4.

## 2.1 Reflections on the Origins of CMC, Vellore

When Ida Sophia Scudder came to visit her parents in Dindivanam (3 hrs travel from Vellore), Ida's father was already a doctor and doing good work. However, the cultural norms of the day did not allow the three men who came to seek medical help for their wives at labour. Probably, we can trace this inspirational event to the lack of education during that time (1890s), the lack of female doctors and other factors. In our country and in many other countries, similar efforts have been taken by many people to bring forth healing and wholeness. This ministry removes the gulf between healthy and the sick, strong and the weak,

## 2.2 A Biblical background of 'being together'

'Being together' and 'staying apart' are mutually opposite aspects of life experience. There are some powerful examples of being together in the scripture. Climbing up is equal to going apart, coming down is equal to being together. In the scripture we have many events where this concept of being together is highlighted.

Jesus in the garden of Gethsemane was pleading with His disciples 'to be with Him' and 'to remain with Him'. During the life and ministry of Jesus, efforts made by our Lord to be with Zacchaeus, Samaritan woman and other common people is indicative of Jesus' mission to be with the humanity. Many of the teachings of Jesus focus on the fact we are called to a life of togetherness.

In the Hebrew Bible, we have so many references where YHWH demonstrated His desire with everyone – both high and low. His dealings with an ordinary group of people like Israelites was indicative of His commitment to this ministry of being together.

## 3. Therapeutic Methods followed by Healthcare Institutions

Different institutions adopt different methods to bring forth healing to people. Particularly the Christian institutions keep Christ as the centre of their thinking and methods. In this section, I would like to highlight few aspects of the life and ministry of Christian Medical College, Vellore. CMC talks much about the combination of training, service and research as important aspects of its existence.

## 3.1 Training of Healthcare professionals in CMC

Right at its inception, CMC has the training of the healthcare professionals in its centre of thinking. In fact, training women was the starting point. It chooses to train candidates from different sections of the society. The sponsorship pattern for the different training programmes are set in such a way people from different sections of the society find an opportunity to get in. The sponsoring churches by and large choose to work among the downtrodden, and therefore it is made easy.

During the training itself, the trainees get a chance to minister to people from different sections of the society: rich and poor, people from different religious backgrounds, learned and illiterate and so on. In other words, the trainees are trained to understand and serve people from different backgrounds. This is an important method of 'being together'. Many under training understand that we are in the process of building God's Kingdom – facilitating people to experience *shalom*.

One part of the training for the students in CMC is their posting in the secondary hospitals in India. These mission hospitals provide training to the students in their own settings in such a way the trainees understand and experience what is the pain of the people in the margins. They try to provide healthcare in the midst of brokenness and suffering.

## 3.2 Healthcare Service in CMC

I would like to highlight some aspects which demonstrate the attempts to bring forth healing and wholeness to people. The emphasis on the community health and villages helps a Christian mission hospital do demonstrate its faith foundation on a triune God who is in communion within the Godhead. To maintain a big establishment like CMC, we need sufficient financial resources. Some people have to be charged in private rates which means the costs they have to bear is comparable to the corporate hospitals in our country. This differential costing of the services provided gives us an opportunity to serve the economically poor friends in a fraction of the actual cost.

The Low Cost Effective Care Unit is set up to care particularly for the urban poor. There are many professionals and trainees who experience 'being together' with the people who come for healthcare needs. It is good for our salvific experience.

I would like to talk about one small event which comes to our attention often. Many from different faiths come to the worship service in the hospital chapel. Whenever there is holy communion, seeing the christians who come for the communion, others also come to kneel down and receive communion. Those of us who are familiar with the church regulations and practice will normally deny to give the sacraments to them. However, sometimes we do ask whether they believe in the Lord Jesus Christ as they are kneeling for the communion. If they affirm, we do give holy sacraments to them also. Do they really believe in the way a church going christian believes or not is not our main concern. I believe this is an attempt to experience the oneness with others in the Lord Jesus Christ in a healing ministry setting.

I would like to highlight another aspect here too. It is a practice mingled with the culture of our nation. Lighting candles and offering incense has been in line with the Indian religious practices. We had few fire incidents due to the candle stand which was kept at the entrance of the main chapel. Therefore, the candle stand was removed from there and kept about 30 metres away from the chapel. The stand was constructed in such a way that it has close resemblance to the grotto of the catholic churches. There is a cross at the top of the grotto. There are many who stand there in front of this for a moment and say a prayer, light a candle, put a garland, offer some incense or lie prostrate so devoutly without being distracted by others nearby. There has been constant criticism from many christian brothers and sisters that this should not be allowed in a christian hospital. However, it is important to note that everyone who stands there irrespective of their religion offer their prayers to Lord Jesus only. This is another attempt to be with others in our attempt to fulfil the last commission of our Lord.

### 3.3 Healthcare Research in CMC

Bioethics is a developing discipline in CMC. One question bioethics asks in many situations is justice and fairness. The very basic of this question is oneness with the people or being together with others. Growing is not as important as growing together. When we do health research we do special attention the bioethical principles like beneficence, non-maleficence, autonomy and justice. Even though we are called to be the leaders of healthcare in our country, there is a constant attempt to make sure that this is done with the whole community in mind holding the human dignity so high. I have seen the members of Ethics committee, Animal Ethics committee, Stem cell Ethics committee and Clinical Ethics committee who take their role so seriously and conscientiously with the clear awareness that we are together with the nature in this whole universe.

Being a pastoral counselor, I would like to add a note regarding the ministry of presence which we counselors practise on a regular basis. Pastoral counselor is a member of the healthcare team. Both in the families and in the society there are people who would like to run faster than others. This causes chaos, discord and hurt in the community and individuals. Therefore, we are called to bring harmony and peace among people and in families. Counselors facilitate people being together and experience love and peace. Bringing the presence of the Almighty in the midst of the conversation sensitively, respectfully and appropriately is also the God-given task of a pastoral counselor in this process.

I am aware that this is more of some random thoughts than an organised scholarly presentation. However, the purpose of this sharing is to communicate how we in a hospital are trying to fulfil the great commission of our Lord and how we experience 'being together' in the midst of brokenness and pain.

*Chapter 9*

# BEING TOGETHER
## IN-BETWEEN BEHIND AND BEYOND

**Mervin Shinoj Boas**[1]

*A good disposition is the only permanent foundation of and guarantee of permanent goodness.*

— B. R. Ambedkar

## 1. Prescript: Process of *Locating* Explored

Where do I want to locate myself? *Behind* or *Beyond* or *In-between.* This is an important question that relocates, restructures, reconstructs, and deconstructs me always. The intensity of this process may vary from time to time as per the demand of the context and on the basis of equipping myself to respond to the need of the context. Locating myself at a particular space is always a challenging process that brings difference on perception, attitude, conviction, response, and epistemological position. Many a time I (the first person remains as a symbolic representative) locate myself *behind.* But rest of the time I want to be *beyond.* Locating in these positions needs to be analyzed epistemologically.

1 Rev. Dr. Mervin Shinoj Boas is an Associate Professor in the Department of Theology and Ethics at the United Theological College, Bangalore.

## 2. Locating *Behind:* Position Deconstructed

In order to being *behind* there is a need to put the factors or events in front. In other words, there is a need to hide behind the reality. In this process, I would locate myself at last and put all facts or events before me. Therefore, the factors or events would be placed in front of me. Everyone will see only the events or incidents at a glance and there is a need for an intentional effort to find out me since I am placed myself behind the reality. Lack of transparency is the problem here. The perpetuator is behind, while the events are highlighted. This is a phenomenon in the process of colonialism. The real maker is vanished. It is very difficult to have access directly to the masters of events. They are not revealed by themselves and always would like to be hidden before society and people due to maintaining the status quo of the hidden agenda.

Further, reason or cause or purpose or intention is hidden by highlighting the layers of events. Therefore, society will be stuck with the event or incident. In other words, cause is not revealed in order to keep the society to be stuck up with event and its consequences. In this state, society cannot reach out to the real cause and intention because of its hidden nature and because of blocking with the effects and consequences or results. In short, the real intention is hidden due to its power of victimization and dehumanization.

Further, the real makers of events do not want to be revealed directly before society. Therefore, agents are appointed to show up themselves as the responsible reasons of events. These agents appear to pretend to behave or act as perpetuators. In this process in society, most of the time the victimized, do not have a direct access to the real perpetuators. At the same time, understanding the fake perpetuators as real and making encounters only with them brings nothing in effect. In this phenomenon, the real masters of events will be safe and comfortable for implementing their secret and exploitative agenda in society. Thus, the phenomenon of remaining behind is a hiding process and at the same time the easiest way of implementing the hidden agenda through the agents. Therefore, if there are any unexpected bad consequences, the agents will be victimized and the real masters will be safe. This is the way the masters keep themselves safe but the agents and people or society stand victimized. This is a process of colonialism.

## 3. Locating *Behind*: A Colonial Discourse

Locating *behind* is acknowledged as a colonial process due to its methods of implementation. The cultural and political notion of globalization and liberalization make more space to locate *behind*. Firstly, the real makers or masters of events are hidden by themselves by locating themselves *behind* for the sake of implementing the secret agenda and to protect themselves from the bad consequences if there is anything arising of it unexpectedly. Secondly, by appointing agents to reveal themselves before the society as perpetuators and responsible persons of events and making them responsible to take care of bad consequences and putting them to be victimized, is further a colonial trend. Thirdly, highlighting the events is the best way for hiding the makers and masters and the real agenda. The society is thus made to be only bothered about the events instead of bothering about real makers who are the real cause of events. In this process, the master of events remains neutral and safe. Fourthly, people are victimized without knowing what is really happening around them. They do not have a direct access to the real masters of events and the real purpose of events. They are given only fake perpetuators to interact. All these actions belong to the process of colonialism. It thus employs the dominant imperialistic social relations as the way to obstruct the real intention, which is brilliantly observed by Gandhi.[2]

## 4. Locating *Beyond:* Understandings Re-considered

The other option is to take a position of *beyond*. To a certain extent it is just opposite the process of locating *behind*. In this method, instead of putting the factors or events in front and staying behind it, a deep critical approach and analysis of factors and events will be taking place and to go ahead to locate in front of the same in the process. However, revisiting, reanalyzing, reconstructing, deconstructing, and restructuring are needed in the process of critical analysis of this situation. Locating myself in front of the events and re-reading through different perspectives is very much appreciated in this method. Usually it is being done by the colonized or the victimized. Many a time, past is the source of this analysis. Further, there is a purposeful attempt to identify the modern forms of dehumanizing structures. Locating in front of events and factors through deep critical analysis reveals the person who does that before the society. Therefore, a kind of transparency exists. The masters who remake the history through "re" and "de" process reveal themselves but they place themselves not with the factors but put them behind. They overtake the events to place themselves in front of the same.

## 5. Locating *Beyond:* A Postcolonial Glaze

Postcolonial methods are always placed *beyond* the colonial methods. 'Being with' is not the method here but *beyond* through a critical analysis. Here, the position of *Beyond* is identified as a postcolonial method due to the following reasons. (i) Makers of events are revealed by themselves before the society. (ii) Nothing is placed by the master of events in front of them to hide themselves. (iii) No hidden agenda is kept for dehumanizing the society. (iv) Real intention or purpose of event is revealed openly. (v) Agents are not appointed to present themselves as perpetuators of events before the society. (vi) Agents and people in the society are not victimized or exploited or colonized. (vii) Direct access to the real makers of

---

2 George Zachariah. *Alternatives Unincorporated: Earth Ethics from the Grassroots* (London, Oakville: Equinox, 2011), p. 105.

facts is possible. (viii) "Re" and "De" processes take place for analyzing critically the past and the present. (ix) The makers of events express themselves as responsible and sincerely committed. (x) Sincere intention for the well-being of society is expressed, especially seeking the real identity and state of the vulnerable. These are acknowledged as the process of postcolonialism.

Since *Being Together* for fulfilling the great mission is the need of the hour, it is not met in these *Behind* or *Beyond* spacing or locating methods. To answer the questions Why? and How?, both the methods should be analyzed from a different perspective.

## 6. *Being Together:* Locating *Behind* or *Beyond* Questioned

The methods of *behind* and *beyond* do not provide a possibility for *being together* with reality. In the method of being *behind,* the real makers and masters are hidden behind. They are not with the real factors and events. Therefore, being together with reality is not possible. They keep themselves away from social actualities. It means that while social realities of the people exist, the *behind masters* want to colonize the actual realities of the people. Therefore, they cannot be with the people. Thus, the method of *Being together* is broken.

In the process of being *beyond,* we have to keep the facts or events behind. That means taking a position to be in front of reality. Analyzing the reality and taking over the same in order to go ahead is the actual process that takes place in this method. This position also does not provide the possibility of being with the reality. In short, *being together* is not possible in this method too.

But, unfortunately most of the time most of the people locate themselves either *behind* or *beyond.* The result is that a majority of the people are not with on in touch with the social reality. But *being together* is claimed, but it may happen in an unreal manner due to staying behind or beyond. Those who decide to be behind will be in a state of being together and those who decide to be beyond also may be having a fellowship of being together. But all these persons are not with reality by putting the real facts or events in front or back. *Being together* with reality is thus expected to explore the real realities of the society. But the position of *behind* or *beyond* do not provide this exploration of reality because it does not provide space for the real state of *being together.*

The problem that has to be noted here is that if we cannot be with the realities of context, we cannot acknowledge the real mission that has to be accomplished. Since we locate ourselves behind or beyond we do not know the realities of the people. Therefore, we fail to identify the real mission. Being together with the people and society is the only way for identifying the urgent needs of the society only from which we can construct contextual missiological methods for fulfilling the great mission. Now the question is, How can we can fulfill the great mission since the method of *behind* or *beyond* are not capable enough to provide the state of *being together*?

supplementary and complementary. The *in-between* position upholds the reality of inclusive pluralism[7] and stands against all kinds of anti-dialogical positions.[8]

**Structural Realm:** "Religion plays a powerful role both in justifying oppression and in inspiring and sustaining thirst, and struggles, for justice."[9] It is, for me, true because religions in India are bothered only about the victims but not bothered about the dehumanizing structures that produce victims. There can be two methods here. One is focusing only on the victims. The other option is focusing only on the dehumanizing structures. Both methods are insufficient to solve the issue. Both the approaches, leave out either the structures that produce victims or victims who are in urgent need, thus both are partial. The former is the method of *behind* because of highlighting events more than the real cause or reason and the latter is the method of *beyond* due its focus only on re-structuring or re-framing the structures and does not bother about the victims. But taking care of victims and at the same time encountering the dehumanizing structure for structural change simultaneously is the best approach to solve the problem. This is the position of *in-between*. This method gives space for *being together* with the victims and at the same time with the structures. The possibility of accomplishing this great mission, i.e., transforming the society, is intact there.

**Trans-national Realm:** Of late, boundaries of nations are strengthened and border issues have emerged enormously in the present context of war and nuclear conflicts. Focusing on the step issues of other nations and keeping secretly all the issues of one's own nation is a dangerous which falls on the method of being *behind*. Highlighting the power and the strength of own nation by putting all other nations behind is also dangerous as it promotes the method of being *beyond*. Both of them bring national conflicts. Revealing the real position and the policies of own nation and interacting with other nations with transparency is the wonderful state of *in-between*.

**Christological Realm:** Focusing on the Jesus of history by staying behind ith Christ of faith or vice versa (behind method) and moving ahead with Christ faith and sidelining Jesus of history or vice versa (beyond method) are not to proposed but holding both together is good for balancing the Christological victions (in-between method). This Christological stand tries to avoid thereby Christological tensions between these notions.

---

gnatius Puthiadam. "Dialogue – Its Basis in Reality" in *Christian Contribution to Indian Philosophy*, edited by Anand Amaladass (Madras: Christian Literature Society, 1995), pp. 127-8.

rghese Manimala. "The Method of the Subalterns: A Study Based on Paulo Freire and nbedkar" in *Philosophical Methods: Through the Prevalent to a Relevant*, edited by Johnson Puthenpurackal. Association of Christian Philosophers of India Series 5 (Bangalore: Asian ding Corporation, 2004), p. 177.

iaan Wielenga, "Liberation Theology in Asia" in *The Cambridge Companion to Liberation logy*, edited by Christopher Rowland (Cambridge, United Kingdom: Cambridge rsity Press, 1977), p. 42.



## 7. Narrating an Example

In the process of crucifixion of Jesus, Judas Iscariot is only an agent but he is revealed as the prime mover of the event. He was only a front. The real maker of the event, the Roman Empire, is hidden, locating itself behind the act. This is the method of being *behind*. The Roman Empire keeps everything else in front of it in order to hide itself due to its secret agenda and thus to maintain ambiguity. As we have discussed earlier, in this process the agents will be victimized. Judas Iscariot was thus a victim since he appeared to be the maker of the event but actually he was not.

Further, Pontius Pilate takes a position of *beyond* the event. By washing his hands off the event, he overcame the facts of the events and put everything behind and tried to go ahead.

But Jesus Christ stands *in-between*. He does not put anything either in the front to hide Himself to have a position of *behind* or backside in order to make Himself *beyond* but He is being with reality, i.e., the real position of *being together*. The true intention on the method of *being together* with people in order to fulfill the great mission is thus exposed by Jesus Christ. The Roman Empire cannot be with the society since taking a position of *behind* the event and Pontius Pilate also cannot be with the reality keeping a position of *beyond* the event. But Jesus Christ is with reality through and there by maintaining a position of being *in-between* that makes everyone to be *being together* with the social realities. For Jesus Christ, nothing there was to put in the front to hide Himself or to put behind, to go ahead without fulfilling the mission. Jesus Christ was *in-between* in order to fulfill the great mission by *being together* with His community. The method of locating onself *in-between* is constructed here.

## 8. Locating *In-between*: Position Re-encountered

Dietrich Bonhoeffer brilliantly explores the position of *in-between* in his book *Creation and Fall: A Theological Exposition of Genesis 1-3*.[3] He elucidates that no one can have a position *at first* or *at last*. It means that you are not the beginner or the ender of anything. You are not even the beginner of your own thought or argument and at the same time it does not stop with you but continues. Therefore, you cannot be either beginner or ender. Your position is always *in-between*. Nobody can be the beginner of anything since everything is in the process of developing. You cannot be the ender since there is no state of perfection. Bonhoeffer explicates that everyone is always in the *middle*.

Our thinking process also is limited with this notion of *in-between*. "Thinking can never answer its own last question," because the thinking process lacks

---

3 Dietrich Bonhoeffer, *Creation and Fall: A Theological Exposition of Genesis 1-3* (Minneapolis: Augsburg Fortress, 1997).

its beginning due to its pattern of circle. Beginning is everywhere in a circle.[4] "Where the beginning begins, there our thinking stops; there it comes to an end." "Beginning is the infinite."[5] Similarly, the end cannot be finite at any cost. Beginning and end are quite open and flexible. Therefore, locating *in-between* is a dynamic process due to its fluid nature.

In the process of *being together*, as we have seen, locating *behind* and *beyond* are incapable within itself. Therefore, locating *in-between* is the correct position in a sense that in this position you or I can be with the reality of the society or with the people through which we would be able to identify the preferential need of the context. This is an urgent step for acknowledging the great mission. Therefore, disposition of the position of *behind* or *beyond* is demanded in order to have a position of *in-between* to provide an organic presence in the society or community.

## 9. Organic Presence: Necessity Expounded

"- - - - - we can never conceive of freedom except in term of necessity."[6] Bonhoeffer quotes the Hegelian idea of Freedom and Necessity which is expounded by Friedrich Brunstad. Since bringing freedom to all living creatures and nature from different bondages or dehumanizing structures is the great universal mission of Christianity, it is very important to trace out the particular urgent demand of particular context in order to construct a missiological method to fulfill the great mission in the context. In this process, *being together* is an unavoidable factor to identify the need in order to materialize the process of establishing freedom in context. *Being together* is the reality of organic presence which should be understood as a sacrificial commitment towards the demand of the community. Wholehearted involvement with the same mind of the people of the context and experiencing pain and suffering of the people with the same intensity of the people and being with them without looking at the consequences is the state of organic presence. In the process of being *behind* or *beyond,* the perpetuators provide a presence but not an organic presence since staying behind or beyond. But the state of *in-between* provides organic presence that brings emancipation to the context. Jesus Christ is thus the role model of the *in-between* state.

Since *being together* can be possible only through the position of *in-between,* the position of *in-between* is not neutral or passive or inactive but active, dynamic and vibrant. *In-between* position does have a clear stand and position with very direct and meaningful purpose and mission.

4 Dietrich Bonhoeffer, *Creation and Fall,* p. 26.

5 Ibid., p. 25.

6 Ibid., p. 26.



## 10. Locating *In-Between:* Postmodernism Re-imagined

All kinds of binarisms are objected by postmodernism. Postmodernism envisions a state where everything is open since nothing is closed. This is so since, everything is in the process of development and nothing is perfect at any point of time. Therefore, new is nothing but a different form of the old. Since, everything is on the move, fluidity is identified as dynamic in nature. Thus, disposition of all static and established positions are promoted by postmodern insights. That means the methods of *behind* and *beyond* are static. But locating at *in-between* is fluid in nature and demands disposition always. The state of *in-between* is open for encountering with the context. The state of freedom or liberation is a social construct as per the necessity of the context. The state of beginning or end is not just a concern of postmodernism but, each and every state is important in the process of development. All these factors, as we have discussed above, can be found in the state of *in- between.* Therefore, location of *in- between* is understood on the ground of postmodern insights.

## 11. *In-Between*: Blazes of Implementation

Trying to understand the location of *in-between* by looking at some crucial realit
of the present context is explored here.

**Self and the Other:** Showing concern towards the Other by placing the
in the front and staying behind is the method of *behind.* Remaining as "sav
or "masters" of the Other by constructing the Other for institutionalizing
the real act of this process. Self is not being with the Other in this proces

Sidelining the Other at behind for expressing Self in the front is th
of *beyond* that occurs almost all the time everywhere. Take a step ahead
the Other which remains behind is the attitude here. Self is not bei
Other in this method.

But, this is done, acknowledging that both the Self and t
inseparable and interdependent in nature as one cannot survive wi
It is the right method of *in-between.* There is thus the Other wit
vice versa, where mutual notions take place. Existence of both
mutual dependence that brings the sense of *being together.* Se
thus a nature of fluidity which is open to both.

**Multi-Religious Realm:** In the context of religious f
fanaticism, putting all other religions in the front and stay
right as it perpetuates inequality. Further, locating *beyond*
also dangerous due to the degrading of other faiths. Bu
brings equality among religions and mutual interacti
are thus possible which is quite good for a multi-relig
promotes uniqueness of each religion since all religic
of society by looking at God through its own uniq
conviction that no religion is contradictory to othe

**Ecological Realm:** There is an on-going debate between development and destruction of nature. Destructing nature for the sake of development and hiding agencies behind the package of development (locating behind) or moving ahead of the process of destructing nature and analyzing it well without interacting with the ecological issues (locating beyond) are meaningless methods. But taking care of nature and environment well and at the same time promoting development (sustainable development) is the right method (locating in-between) that avoids conflicts.

**Theological Realm:** Traditional classical theologies and liberation theologies have their own methodological and hermeneutical frame that do not have enough interaction with each other. Both may have only a *conjuctional Relation.*[10] Placing liberation theologies in the front and the traditional classical theologies behind brings us theological issues (location of behind). Aravind P. Nirmal was frightened of this method as this kind of thinking would place dominant theologies behind and focus on other emerging contextual theologies as a strategic approach to swallow the emerging theologies. Therefore, he proposed "methodological exclusivism" as a hermeneutical method for dalit theology. Going beyond with liberation theologies and placing traditional classical theologies behind also is a ground for theological conflicts (location of beyond) due to its power of degradation. But balancing both the theological notions (in-between method) is appreciated due to its possibility of interaction and mutual developments.

**Gender Realm:** Patriarchy and feminism have been in mutual conflicts. Highlighting feminism by the patriarchy by placing itself behind should be suspected because of establishing the male as the saviour of female. Feminism rejects this method (method of behind). At the same time, highlighting feminism by placing patriarchy behind (method of beyond) is also bringing enmity between them. Taking a position *in-between* by acknowledging the uniqueness and inevitability of both and understanding that one cannot survive without the other brings mutual acceptance and peace between them.

## 12. Postscript: *In-between* Proposed

Locating *behind* or *beyond* has its own structure of degradation, exploitation, and oppression. These methods consist of the process of colonialism or postcolonialism. The problem is that both do not bring solutions but create enmity between them. The position of *in-between* finds solutions to certain extent to the existing issues due to its open and fluid nature. It brings mutual understandings and possibility of interaction on the ground of transparency. For fulfilling the great mission as per the need of context, the *in-between* position is found better.

10 "Conjuction (Samyoga) is a temporary relation of contact between two separate objects", Christopher Bartley, *An Introduction to Indian Philosophy* (London and New York: Continuum, 2011), p. 99.

*Chapter 10*

# 'BEING TOGETHER LIBERATION, JUSTICE, AND PEACE' CONTESTING VOICES AND COMPETING IDENTITIES IN THE INDIAN CHURCH AND SOCIETY

K. Jesurathnam[1]

## I

### Introduction

We are living in more turbulent socio-economic and religio-cultural and political context than our ancestors in the past centuries. Our context is such that we can no longer manage to address the issues and problems of today with our old and set-patterned remedies our ancestors managed to employ to address the problems in the church and society. Brueggemann has rightly summarized this situation regarding US society and is not much different from today's Indian church and society. He writes:

> Our society is marked by a deep dislocation that touches every aspect of our lives. The old certitudes seem less certain; the old privileges are under

1 Rev. Dr. K. Jesurathnam is a Professor in the Department of Biblical Studies at the United Theological College, Bangalore.

> powerful challenge; the old dominations are increasingly ineffective and fragile; the established governmental, educational, judicial and medical institutions seem less and less able to deliver what we need and have come to expect; the old social fabrics are fraying under the assault of selfishness, fear, anger and greed. There seems no going back to our former world, since the circumstances making that world sustainable have changed. Because the church has been intimately connected with the old patterns of certitude, privilege and domination, it shares a common jeopardy with other old institutions. Church members are confused about authority, bewildered about mission, worried about finances, contentious about norms and ethics, and anxious about the church's survival. Our numbed and bewildered society lacks ways of thinking and speaking that can help us find remedies—that can enable us to go deep into the crisis and so avoid denial, and to imagine a better future and so avoid despair. But when the church is faithful to its own past life with God, it has ways of speaking, knowing and imagining that can successfully address our cultural malaise. When it remembers its ancient miracles, has the courage to speak in its own cadences, and re-engages old seasons of hurt, the church possesses the rhetorical and testimonial antidotes to denial and despair.[2]

The above statement is very clear in the light of the dismal performance of the institutionalized church, particularly her performance in the recent times. Our society and social systems are highly skewed and fractured with identity problems and other ethnic conflicts in this century more than ever before. People all over are looking for a proper guidance and a way-out of the crisis that our ecclesial and societal structures have created and thus resulted in a wide gap between the rich and poor, dalits and non-dalits, tribals and non-tribals, men and women, those in the power and powerless, those privileged and under-privileged, those economically better and economically vulnerable and marginalized and so on. Today we are living in the times of self-imposed exile in our church and society more than ever before. It looks as if our present precarious situation will not easily let us come out of our own rigid structures unless we make an earnest effort to address the pressing socio-political, cultural, religious and economic crises and suggest possible ways to deal with our self-imposed or self-created problems.

In the light of the above discussion the task of this presentation is to do the following: first, to gather and present some recent data on our socio-political, religious, cultural and economic issues both in the church and society. Second, to reflect upon the anomalies that we are facing in the above mentioned areas.

2 Walter Brueggemann, "Conversations among Exiles," *The Christian Century*, July 2-9, 1997, p. 630.

Third, suggest ways in which we can avoid more damage to the skewed social and ecclesial systems in order to give a better future for posterity.

## II

## Data on Poverty in India - A Brief Overview

Poverty in India is widespread, and a variety of methods have been proposed to measure it. The official measure of Indian government, before 2005, was based on food security and it was defined from per capita expenditure for a person to consume enough calories and be able to pay for associated essentials to survive. Since 2005, Indian government adopted the Tendulkar methodology which moved away from calorie anchor to a basket of goods and used rural, urban and regional minimum expenditure per capita necessary to survive.

The World Bank has similarly revised its definition and benchmarks to measure poverty since 1990, with $1.25 per day income on purchasing power parity basis as the definition in use from 2005 to 2013. Some semi-economic and non-economic indices have also been proposed to measure poverty in India; for example, the Multi-dimensional Poverty Index placed 33% weight on number of years spent in school and education and 6.25% weight on financial condition of a person, in order to determine if that person is poor.

The different definitions and different underlying small sample surveys used to determine poverty in India, have resulted in widely different estimates of poverty from 1950s to 2010s. In 2012, the Indian government stated 21.9% of its population is below its official poverty limit. The World Bank, in 2011 based on 2005's International Comparison Program, estimated 23.6% of Indian population, or about 276 million people lived below $1.25 per day on purchasing power parity. According to United Nation's Millennium Development Goal programme 270 million or 21.9% people out of 1.2 billion of Indians lived below poverty line of $1.25 in 2011-2012.

Poverty in India is a historical reality. From late 19th century through early 20th century, under British colonial rule, poverty in India intensified, peaking in 1920s. Famines and diseases killed millions each time. After India gained its independence in 1947, mass deaths from famines were prevented, but poverty increased, peaking post-independence in 1960s. Rapid economic growth since 1991, has led to sharp reductions in extreme poverty in India. However, those above poverty line live a fragile economic life. Lack of basic essentials of life such as safe drinking water, sanitation, housing, health infrastructure as well as malnutrition impact the lives of hundreds of millions

The World Bank reviewed and proposed revisions in May 2014, to its poverty calculation methodology and purchasing power parity basis for measuring poverty worldwide, including India. According to this revised methodology, the world had 872.3 million people below the new poverty line, of which 179.6 million people lived in India. In other words, India with 17.5% of total world's population, had 20.6% share of world's poorest in 2011.[3]

**Impact of Poverty – An Overview:** Since the 1950s, the Indian government and non-governmental organizations have initiated several programmes to alleviate poverty, including subsidizing food and other necessities, increased access to loans, improving agricultural techniques and price supports, and promoting education and family planning. These measures have helped eliminate famines, cut absolute poverty levels by more than half, and reduced illiteracy and malnutrition.

Although the Indian economy has grown steadily over the last two decades, its growth has been uneven when comparing social groups, economic groups, geographic regions, and rural and urban areas. Between 1999 and 2008, the annual growth rates for Gujarat, Haryana, or Delhi were much higher than for Bihar, Uttar Pradesh, or Madhya Pradesh. Poverty rates in rural Orissa (43%) and rural Bihar (41%) are among the world's most extreme. Despite significant economic progress, one quarter of the nation's population earns less than the government-specified poverty threshold of ₹ 32 per day (approximately US$ 0.6). According to the 2001 census, 35.5% of Indian households used banking services, 35.1% owned a radio or transistor, 31.6% a television, 9.1% a phone, 43.7% a bicycle, 11.7% a scooter, motorcycle or a moped, and 2.5% a car, jeep or van; 34.5% of the households had none of these assets. According to Department of Telecommunications of India the phone density reached 73.34% by December 2012 and as an annual growth decreased by –4.58%. This tallies with the fact that a family of four with an annual income of ₹ 137000 (US$2,100) could afford some of these luxury items.[4]

**Poverty Among Dalits: An Overview:** If you are a Dalit in India you can expect to have 4 years less to live than others. You can expect more than half of your children to suffer from under-nutrition. One third of the women in your community will be anemic. For every 100 Dalit children born in your community, 12 would already be dead before they reached their fifth birthday. Only 1 out of every 5 children in your community would not drop out of school, and only about half would even become literate despite that fact that around 2/3 of Indians are literate. You would have less than 1 in 600 chance of gaining a postgraduate diploma (if you are a women, make that 1 in 1,200). You have an unemployment rate of 5% compared to 3.5% for others, you are half as likely to have fixed capital assets and four times as likely to become a bonded laborer, joining the estimated 24.4 million other Dalit bonded labourers. One in every three in your community will be poor while the 'touchable' communities will have a 4 in 5 chance of escaping poverty. Government's policy is supposed to not only reduce Dalit poverty, but also to reduce the staggering gap between Dalits and non-Dalits. This policy is failing. While poverty generally is reducing in India, the main

3 http:// www.en.wikipedia.org/wiki/Poverty_in_India accessed on September 26, 2015.

4 Ibid.

beneficiaries are non-dalits. It has been estimated that both cities and rural areas, the gap between Dalits and non-Dalits has been increasing since at least the early 1990s. The increasing gap between the untouchable castes and the dominant castes is more than just number-crunching: it also represents an increase in the relative power of dominant castes to exploit the Dalits in neighboring villages. Dalits and slums Caste discrimination is often thought of as a purely rural phenomenon, but official slum data alone show that this is not the case. 79.8% of Dalits live in rural India. Their over-representation in rural India means that they only account for 11.78% of India's urban population. However, they are highly over-represented in the 'official' slums of Indian cities, where they make up 17.4% of the population, or 7.4 million Dalits. Since Dalits are not highly present in the recognized slums of Mumbai, if we look at some of the major cities of India we see even greater disproportions in the number of Dalits living in slums with almost one third of slum dwellers in Chennai, Delhi and Bangalore being Dalits.[5]

## Caste Based Discrimination – An Overview

While poverty seems to have been showing the declining trend, other forms of discrimination continue to increase in the Indian church and society. One such stark reality can be noted in caste and gender discrimination. Women and children in particular are the worst victims of the skewed socio-economic system in India. Poverty is also associated with the marginal and vulnerable groups in this regard. Most Dalits in India continue to live in extreme poverty, without land or opportunities for better employment or education. With the exception of a minority who have benefited from India's policy of quotas in education and government jobs, Dalits are relegated to the most menial of tasks as removers of human waste and dead animals, leather workers, street sweepers, and cobblers. Dalit children make up the majority of children sold into bondage to pay off debts to upper-caste creditors.

According to government statistics, an estimated one million Dalits in India are "manual scavengers" (a majority of them women) who clear feces from public and private latrines and dispose of dead animals; unofficial estimates are much higher. Handling of human waste is a caste-based occupation, deemed too "polluting and filthy" for anyone but Dalits. Manual scavengers exist under different caste names throughout the country, such as the Bhangis in Gujarat, the Pakhis in Andhra Pradesh, and the Sakkaliars in Tamil Nadu. Members of these communities are invariably placed at the very bottom of the caste hierarchy, and even the hierarchy of Dalit sub-castes. Using little more than a broom, a tin plate, and a basket, they are made to clear feces from public and private latrines and carry waste to dumping grounds and disposal sites. Though long outlawed, the practice of manual scavenging continues in most states. The poor remuneration of

5 http:// www.en.wikipedia.org/wiki/Poverty_in_India accessed on September 26, 2015.

manual scavenging, agricultural labor, and other forms of low-caste employment often force families of lower castes or caste-like groups into bondage. A lack of enforcement of relevant legislation prohibiting debt bondage in most of the countries concerned allows for the practice to continue unabated.

An estimated forty million people in India, among them some fifteen million children, are working in slave-like conditions in order to pay off debts as bonded laborers. Due to the high interest rates charged, the employers' control over records, and the abysmally low wages paid, the debts are seldom settled. Bonded laborers are frequently low-caste, illiterate, and extremely poor, while the creditors/employers are usually higher-caste, literate, comparatively wealthy, and relatively more powerful members of the community.[6]

Over fifty years since India's constitutional promise of free, compulsory, primary education for all children up to the age of fourteen-with special care and consideration to be given to promote the educational progress of scheduled castes-illiteracy still exists among almost two-thirds of the Dalit population as compared to about one-half of the general population. The literacy gap between Dalits and the rest of the population fell a scant 0.39% between 1961 and 1991. Most of the government schools in which Dalit students are enrolled are deficient in basic infrastructure, classrooms, teachers, and teaching aids. A majority of Dalit students are also enrolled in vernacular schools whose students suffer serious disadvantages in the job market as compared to those who learn in English-speaking schools. Despite state assistance in primary education, Dalits also suffer from an alarming drop-out rate. According to the *National Commission for Scheduled Castes and Scheduled Tribes' 1996-1997 and 1997-1998 Report*, the national drop-out rate for Dalit children-who often sit in the back of classrooms-was a staggering 49.35% at the primary level, 67.77% for middle school, and 77.65% for secondary school.[7]

## The Plight of Dalit Women-thrice Alienated

Lower-caste women are singularly positioned at the bottom of caste, class, and gender hierarchies. Largely uneducated and consistently paid less than their male counterparts worldwide they invariably bear the brunt of exploitation, discrimination, and physical attacks. Sexual abuse and other forms of violence against women are often used by landlords and the police to inflict political "lessons" and crush dissent within the community. Lower-caste women also suffer disproportionately in terms of access to health care, education, and subsistence wages as compared to women of higher castes.

Dalit women in India make up the majority of landless laborers and scavengers, as well as a significant percentage of the women forced into prostitution in rural areas or sold into urban brothels. As such, they come into greater contact with

6 http://www.hrw.org/reports/2001/globalcaste/caste0801-03.htm (accessed on September 19, 2015).

7 Ibid.

landlords and enforcement agencies than their upper-caste counterparts. Their subordinate position is exploited by those in power who carry out their attacks with impunity. Incidents of gang-rape, stripping, and parading women naked through the streets, and making them eat excrement are all crimes specific to Dalit women in India. Sexual violence is also linked to debt bondage in India.[8]

According to a Tamil Nadu state government official, the rape of Dalit women exposes the hypocrisy of the caste system as "no one practices untouchability when it comes to sex." Like other Indian women whose relatives are sought by the police, Dalit women have also been arrested and tortured in custody as a means of punishing their male relatives who are hiding from the authorities. Dalit women are economically marginalized and exploited, both within and outside their families. As the largest group of those engaged in manual labor and agricultural production, their jobs often include waste disposal, clearing carcasses, and doing leatherwork. Despite their grueling tasks and long hours, exploitative wages ensure that Dalit women are unable to earn a subsistence living. In some rural areas Dalit women scarcely earn ten to twenty kilograms of food grain a year, barely enough to sustain a family. Many have been driven to prostitution. One caste in particular, known as *badis,* is viewed as a prostitution caste. Many Dalit women and girls, including those from the *badi* caste, are trafficked into sex work in Indian brothels. Under the devadasi system, thousands of Dalit girls in India's southern states are ceremonially "dedicated" or married to a deity or to a temple. Once dedicated, they are forced to become prostitutes for upper-caste community members, and eventually auctioned into an urban brothel.[9]

## Untouchability Still Practiced in India

In the so called developing nation like India, where can one see untouchability? A 2006 study on untouchability rural in India covering 565 villages in 11 States has revealed the extent to which Untouchability – officially banned under the 1950 Constitution – continues to be the daily reality for millions of Indians. In government services despite being charged with a constitutional mandate to promote social justice, various local institutions of the Indian State clearly tolerate and even facilitate the practice of untouchability. In 37.8% of the villages Dalits are made to sit separately in government schools. In 27.6% of the villages Dalits are prevented from entering police stations. In 25.7% of the villages Dalits are prevented from entering ration shops. In 33% of the villages public health workers refuse to visit Dalit homes. In 23.5% of the Dalit villages don't get mail delivered to their homes. In 14.4% of the Dalit villages Dalits are not permitted to enter the 'panchayat' Local Government building. In 12% of the Dalit villages Dalits denied access to or forced to form separate lines at polling booths. In 48.4%

8 http://www.hrw.org/reports/2001/globalcaste/caste0801-03.htm (accessed on September 19, 2015).

9 Ibid.

of the Dalit villages they are denied access to water sources. In Market Access 35% of villages surveyed: Dalits barred from selling produce in local markets; 47% of villages with milk cooperatives prevent Dalits from selling milk, and 25% prevent Dalits from buying milk. In work 25% of villages: Dalits paid lower wages than non-Dalits, work longer hours, have more delayed waged and suffer more verbal and physical abuse. In 37% of villages Dalit workers are paid wages from a distance to avoid physical contact. In Religion and Rites 64% of Dalits are restricted from entering Hindu temples. In almost 50% of villages Dalits are prevented from accessing cremation grounds. In the Private Sphere in 73% of villages Dalits are not permitted to enter non-Dalit homes. In 70% of villages Dalits and non-Dalits cannot eat together. In the villages 35.8% of Dalits are denied entry into village shops.[10]

## Atrocities against Dalits

Atrocities against Dalits Atrocities are an official category of crime in India defined by The Scheduled Castes and Scheduled Tribes (Prevention of Atrocities) Act, 1989. The Act defines atrocities as crimes such as: forcing Dalits to eat obnoxious substances, dumping excreta or carcasses in Dalit premises, assaulting a Dalit woman with intent to dishonor or outrage her modesty, using a position of dominance to sexually exploit a Dalit woman, parading Dalits naked or with painted face or body, forcing Dalits to do forced or bonded labour, dispossessing Dalits of their land and forcing Dalits from their homes, preventing Dalits from voting, fouling a Dalit water source, publicly humiliating Dalits, using fire or explosives to damage Dalit property, fabricating evidence in order to convict innocent Dalits. It has been estimated that according to official Indian crime statistics, Dalits are averaged over the period of 2001-2005: 27 atrocities against Dalits every day, 13 Dalits murdered every week, 5 Dalits' homes or possessions burnt every week, 6 Dalits kidnapped or abducted every week, 3 Dalit women raped every day, 11 Dalits beaten every day, A crime committed against a Dalit every 18 minutes.[11]

## How can there be Impunity when the Laws are there?

It has been calculated that some 7,099 or 18.70% of crimes against Dalits were pending with police at the end of 2002. The number of cases pending with the Courts was at the same time 126,009 or 77.69% of all cases brought to court. It appears that only 21.72% of the total cases were disposed of during the year. Out of the disposed cases, 2.31% ended up in conviction. This data has been presented by the Indian Ministry of Social Justice and Empowerment in 2002. But by 2005,

10 http://www.hrw.org/reports/2001/globalcaste/caste0801-03.htm (accessed on September 19, 2015).

11 http://www.dalits.nl/pdf/CastAnEye.pdf (accessed on September 26, 2015).

Indian police statistics show that things had worsened: 23.9% of crimes against Dalits were 'pending investigation' by the police at the end of 2005, 80.2% of crimes against Dalits were 'pending trial' by the courts at the end of 2005.[12]

## Challenges of Fascism and Religious Fundamentalism

Despite all kinds of claims that India is marching ahead in the arena of technology on par with China and other developing nations, the gruesome incidents within the country reflect the backwardness of the state and the resurgence of religious fundamentalism and fascism in vivid forms. People at certain pockets of the country are more intolerant towards other minority religions. In the name of Hindu ideology, sacredness of cow etc some fringe elements leash out violence by stirring up the religious sentiments of the common people and later turn their sentiments as vote banks. Recent incidents in Uttar Pradesh is a clear example of this glaring social reality in today's Indian context. Commenting on the latest developments of religious intolerance, Razu rightly states as follows:

> BJP leaders who have made odious statements such as Sakshi Maharaj, MP belonging to BJP openly and loudly proclaimed that he is ready to kill and be killed to protect the cow. Sangeet Som, a BJP MLA in the Uttar Pradesh Assembly whose role in the terrible 2013 communal violence in Muzaffarnagar and also in western UP and not far from Dadri openly said that the Samajwadi Party's government in UP was protecting "cow eater" because the chief minister met the family of the deceased and offered compensation. Mohan Bhagwat, the RSS chief openly proclaimed India is a Hindu raj. Provocative statements and utterances from these fringe elements appear all the time and should be taken seriously. Nonetheless, their actions are ludicrous and totally bizarre. If a cow is slaughtered, the alleged slaughter is killed and punished. Should the life of any animal be placed above a human life? And who has given the mob the right to take the law into their hands? Although cow slaughter is banned until now there has not been any evidence that Akhlaq and his family had killed a calf and eaten the meat and thus broken the state law. The act of mob lynching and destroying a family is based on floated rumors that seemed to have engineered and thus triggered communal violence. Strategically mobs are deployed so that it becomes difficult to gather evidence against those who perpetrated the communal crime. This has been the strategy these fringe elements always employ. Inciting communal conflagrations before elections has been the grand design of BJP to polarize public opinion and votes.[13]

---

12 http://www.dalits.nl/pdf/CastAnEye.pdf (accessed on September 26, 2015).

13 I. John Mohan Razu, "Pluralism and Tolerant VS Majoritarinism and Intolerant", An unpublished write-up privately circulated on October 9, 2015.

The fear of the many secular ideologues in today's India is that whether the present federal regime is gradually building up a Hindu state as against the secular ideologies enshrined with the fundamental human rights in the Indian constitution. The situation of fascism seems to be on the door step in today's India. Again Razu rightly observes and comments on the present Indian scenario:

> As against the backdrop (of violent incidents in recent times in India like: Dadri lynching. Muzaffarnagar etc.), many questions loom: What message do these incidences convey? Have secularism, pluralism and unity-in-diversity failed? Has the Indian state failed? The intolerance and lynching we have been experiencing and witnessing be considered as traces and semblances of fascism. How to discern the things that are happening around us? Fascism is "like a completely successful operation: the patient dies and all his illusions are removed." So, "fascism is a volatile blend of illusion and reality, the twin qualities being helplessly intertwined, largely incapable either of separation or identification." Usually the fascist politics that the political parties share a common reservoir of frustrations and hatreds, not the least of which is scorn for the values of their civilization. Some keep talking about tolerance and mutual co-existence but the fascists tend to become increasingly intolerant and violent. The civilization and tolerance the fascists mean their brand of civilization and tolerance they subscribe is only to their majoritarian-religious group. It believes in hierarchy primarily in terms of nation as exemplified by the leaders. Similar characteristics we see in RSS leadership which the BJP tows.[14]

In the above light it is our urgent task to take the situation at hand seriously and address the needs of the community in which we are an integral part. We now move on to talk about the Church situation briefly which is not so much different than that of the society. In the light of few biblical and theological reflections we will focus on how to take our responsibility seriously in the precarious situation in which we are compelled to live. Few examples would suffice to make our presentation clear on this important concern.

## III

In the Bible, we do have several texts that unquestionably support the marginalized and underprivileged groups. Several prophetic texts voice out very clearly how God stands in solidarity with the marginalized in ancient Israel. For instance, Jeremiah 43:8-44:30 is an eye opener for all the marginal communities including

14 I. John Mohan Razu, "Fascism is at India's Doorstep'—Reality of a failed state", An unpublished write-up privately circulated on October 10, 2015. The words in the brackets are of the contributor..

Dalits. In this passage when Jeremiah tried to genuinely advise the Judeans in Egypt they resisted the words and advice of the prophet without giving any due regard to such words. They thought that the prophet would simply tune according to what they want rather than being obedient to God's will. Dalits face similar situation like Jeremiah. Whenever Dalits raise voice against any anomalies that exist in the socio-political systems of both the state and the church they are brutally attacked and targeted. They are put into distressing situations by the caste community in order to negate all that they have said and claim. Dalits are charged as rebellious community in the church who disturb the peaceful coexistence of all people in God's kingdom on this earth. The following report written on the caste bias and discrimination Dalits face in the church is a stark reality in today's Indian church.

> By failing to take steps to attain the constitutional protection and safeguards to the dalit Christians from the centuries old social atrocity of "untouchability", the Indian Church has proved herself to be a Caste-based Church who began to neglect the welfare of Dalit Christians even 50 years ago. Even though there are ample reasons to show that Dalit Christians are eligible and deserve the constitutional reservations in education, employment and administrations, the Indian caste-based Church has failed in her duty to use her authority, her institutional, administrative and organizational powers and influence and take steps to reach an accord for it at that time. Thereby, she has caused irreparable loss to the social progress and development of Dalit Christians. The Minority Rights guaranteed by the Indian Constitution has been misused by the Church to safeguard only the interest of the upper Caste -Christians, but at the same time to enslave Dalit Christians and hinder their progress, thereby her administration becoming a structure and instrument of promoting caste oppression and discrimination.
>
> The Indian Catholic Church authorities have refused to lead the administration in the very "noble path of love" preached by Jesus Christ; but instead have adopted only the mean manners of caste-mindedness, hatred and inequalities which were created by the Hindu religion. Since the powers, authority, official posts, organizations and financial resources are all in the absolute hold of the caste-priests, nuns, bishops and the religious, the Dalit Christians are not able to get an equal share for them in education, employment opportunities, welfare and development schemes available in the Church. This has hindered the progress of Dalit Christians for long and has forced them to the situation of fighting for their rights. But the Church authorities are least worried about this. … The Church authorities not only refuse to function on the basis of the

noble values of equality, peace and brotherhood, etc, but also choke the voice of the Dalit Christians who advocate these ideals and try to foster a Christian life in the Church on the basis of these values. For this they misuse their powers authority, influence, money and also the Government machinery such as the Police Department. The Dalit Christians who are in a big majority in the Church do not get a proportionate share in the powers and authority, in admissions and appointments in the educational institutions. The casteist authorities of our institutions, the priests and nuns holding various positions are not willing to concede this even till today. On the contrary, they give most opportunities to the upper caste Christians who are only a minority and continue to justify the same. This is what we call the caste-culture and caste-tradition of the Indian Church. The Dalit Christians struggle is to condemn vehemently these caste domination, oppression, atrocity and betrayal.[15]

The above report clarifies how Dalits face marginalization just as the biblical prophet Jeremiah faced marginalization among the selfish leaders of his time who only promote their selfish interests.

Jer 45:1-5, the last passage of this section can be well related to Dalit context. In the midst of continuous oppression and assaults they face in the hands of caste community Dalits are desperate in seeking "rest" and "great things" from God and even at times God's "mighty acts" and thus they even believe that the deliverance comes to them in a mighty way from God. It is not an unreasonable expectation on the part of Dalits given the context in which they struggle and toil all through their life. Like Baruch and Jeremiah they express words of despair and anguish. One such voice is expressed as follows:

Speaking on the point a pioneering Dalit theologian A. P. Nirmal sums up the integral link between Jesus' sufferings on the cross as the rejected person with that of Dalit experience in the contemporary world. Nirmal's states:

> On the cross, He was the broken, the crushed, the split, the torn, the driven-asunder man—the dalit in the fullest possible meaning of that term. "My God, my God, why hast thou forsaken me?" He cries aloud from the cross. The Son of God feels that He is God-forsaken. That feeling of being God-forsaken is at the heart of our dalit experiences

15 The following article was published by Dr.Mary John, president of DCLM before the arrival of our Holy Father John Paul II to India in November 1999) under the title: "Dalit Christians' Accusation against Casteist Hierarchical Church Authorities in India," and it can be accessed on the site: http://www.dalitchristians.com/html/dalitaccusation.htm (accessed on April 30, 2014).

> and dalit consciousness in India. It is the dalitness of the divinity and humanity that the cross of Jesus symbolizes.[16]

Reflecting on the violence meted out to Dalit and Black women, a feminist Dalit theologian observes:

> A woman hanging upside down, as if to be roasted for the next meal! Kauser Bano is captured to satiate the "hunger" of violence by the mob. So also is the nameless Black woman. Perhaps their scream of helplessness like that of Jesus: 'My God, My God, why did you forsake me', is drowned by the noise of violence around them.... (They also cry) "My God, My God, don't forsake your children who need courage/strength from you".[17]

The above two quotes sufficiently explain the amount of despair and despondency Dalits express looking at their pathetic situation. But like Jeremiah and Baruch who received God's promise of life in the midst of assaults and death, God's enduring promise of life is also given to Dalits. In this way Dalits, Jeremiah and Baruch live in solidarity with one another as their life on this earth stands as a living witness to God's faithfulness in their lives.

Another important aspect emerges from Jere 43:8-44:30 is the case of Babylon. God has consistently attacked Babylon on account of her pride and arrogance. In all possible ways God punished the pride of Babylon in order that everyone will know how the Lord is sovereign and the great monster is controlled by God. In the same manner, God would punish the oppressive caste community in order that they will be humiliated as long as they continue to oppress Dalits. The prayers cited below express similar concern on Dalit hope and aspiration in God's marvelous deeds as happened in the life of Mary.

> So can we identify the Mary of the Incarnation with the hope of a new life for the Dalit woman of today? Mary could so easily have become the target of injustice just as the Dalit women, in spite of all the promises, probably still suffer today. Mary's fears were unfounded where Joseph was concerned and so, presumably she was still an accepted member of her society. As we have seen in the poem 'I am the Mary of your Christmas cards', this didn't mean all her troubles would be over but she knew in her heart what Jesus life on earth was all about. He had been sent by God to redeem the world. You and me, the Dalit women and the whole of the human race. The Christian Dalit women will, no doubt, hear once again

---

16 Arvind P. Nirmal, "Towards a Christian Dalit Theology," in R. S. Sugirtharajah (ed) *Frontiers in Asian Christian Theology*, (Maryknoll: Orbis Books, 1994), p. 39.

17 Evangeline Anderson-Rajkumar, "Politicising the Body: A Feminist Christology," *Asia Journal of Theology* 18:1 (2004), p. 92.

> this Christmas the words of the Magnificat as we have done today. Let us try to imagine what significance they must have for them as we sing the wonderful words in the hymn version which begins with the letter!'
>
> Abuse, yes that's what I get daily. I am frightened of being abducted like some of the young girls from our village. This caste system started with the Hindu religion but it has infected the Christian Church yes, I am a Christian. I try to hold my head high when these attacks come because I know Jesus loves me and cares about what I go through every day. I try to turn away and not hear the words of scorn. I try to pray for my abusers but it is hard when nothing seems to improve for us.
>
> Mary: Injustice, that's what my society is full of. When the neighbours and my childhood friends won't even listen let alone believe my story it feels so unjust. They are supposed to be good Jews, too, waiting for the Messiah but now He is promised - that's different. I am to blame for my situation. But, I have to believe that I am going to bear God's Son, He is to be Incarnate through me. Dalit: I believe I have some good news to tell you. I believe our prayers may have been answered. Injustice to some degree may be over for us. Yes, we walked a long way but before we reached Delhi the government promised that we would be given land on which to make a living, some forest land and access to water. We will need to help them keep us in mind but it sounds more hopeful. Inequality is so wrong for, as Christians, we believe we are all made in the image of God.[18]

The text of Jer 43:8-44:30 also talks about the punishment of Babylon which ushers in a new age of restoration for Judah whereby she will be homecoming and resettle in her own land. Dalit hope and aspiration is rooted in their firm belief that God in Jesus Christ will redeem them and restore them to normal situation where they live in dignity and self-worth. They envisage such a place where everyone is equal and the caste is totally annihilated. The following quote illustrates the significance of Jesus standing in solidarity with the Dalit brothers and sisters in a way that brings them liberation from caste and other associated evils of oppression.

> Jesus' dalitness is symbolized at its best on the cross. It is on the cross that we see Him as the broken one, the one crushed, rejected, cast out of the city - a true dalit. He hangs on the cross exposing the highest measure of dehumanization.

18 The following prayers are taken from the source: www.mwib.org.uk/.../dalit.../249_ee4ea3933295b07787b7d4baa2dec56... (accessed on May 13, 2014).

> The cross is also the price He had to pay for His identification with the dalits - His solidarity with the poor and the outcasts and His confrontation with the powerful that oppress them Here I think, the dalits could be motivated for social change. They should be made to realize that their misery and injustice is not God given - it is manmade - and it can and must be changed. We can show Jesus as the one who fought to bring down the unjust social structure. Just as Jesus had to take up the cross and die in the process of establishing social justice - the dalits must be prepared for sacrifices and even loss of lives in order to restore their honor and dignity. But their struggle for liberation must go on.
>
> Many Dalit Theologians would identify the cry of Jesus on the cross, 'My God, My God why have you forsaken me" (Mt. 27:46-47) as one of the most authentic dalit experiences. The experience of God-forsakenness is a common and inevitable feeling of the dalits. Sometimes, God seems to be so far away - He doesn't seem to care. One can meaningfully convey to the dalits that Jesus has experienced this authentically dalit emptiness. Just as the people mocked and ridiculed Jesus the dalits may become a laughing stock or an abomination in the eyes of the public. But Jesus tells them that even at the thick of the God forsakenness He was certain that God would vindicate Him and help Him achieve His mission. The same compassionate God (though the dalits cannot see the compassion many times - they feel they suffer alone) will certainly vindicate the dalit community.
>
> The Resurrection is the vindication of the mission of Jesus. This can be a tremendous sign of hope for the dalits that they could in fact realize their dream of equality and justice. The risen Jesus is still with them encouraging them and strengthening them to continue their fight against injustice and oppression. By rising from the dead Jesus proved that death is not the last word. Evil and injustice cannot and will not have the final victory. This gives hope to the dalits that their struggle against injustice and oppression is not a lost battle. They will see the light of day. They will be able to rise with Jesus to a more human existence.[19]

In a quite unimaginable and surprising ways Jesus' image as a Dalit living in solidarity with the Dalits is a great boon to the restoration of Dalits in terms of shattering the great monster of caste system but also giving them hope of eternal salvation from the caste oppression. Thus, Dalit Christology affirms that God in Jesus Christ has vindicated the cause of Dalits by liberating them from the

19 Taken from the source: www.dalitchristians.com/html/Jesus%20and%20Dalit.doc (accessed on May 13, 2014).

bondage of caste evils and providing them a space in the wider salvific plan of God as humans with worth and self-respect.

## IV

## Concluding Remarks

In the light of the foregoing discussion on the glaring socio-political and ecclesial reality in India today and the apparent social and cultural inequality both in the church and society, we now conclude this presentation with the following observations and comments:

First, in the world of competing identities minority communities like Dalits, tribals, children and women should continue their quest for seeking full humanity. Their contesting voices can never be stopped until the day when they achieve the target.

Second, not only in India but throughout the world we see similar tendencies of segregation and marginalization on the basis of racism, zionism and casteism. The Blacks are discriminated on the basis of racism, Palestinians are discriminated on the basis of Zionism and Dalits are discriminated on the basis of casteism. Thus, the oppressed communities can be found in the entire global context. Their fight against the oppression is an ongoing struggle against the hegemonic structures all over the world.

Third, it would be wise for the political leaders and the policy makers in every country to make plans and implement them on the basis of poverty, and other socio-political, religious and cultural disparities rather than boasting about progress in terms of modernization, scientific and technological advancements.

Fourth, the church which is part and parcel of the society, instead of becoming an oppressive community, must join in solidarity with all those who cry for justice in order to alleviate poverty and other forms of oppression so that an emergence of just and egalitarian human society will be realized on this earth here and now.

## Chapter 11

# RE-VISITING THE ECUMENICAL PRIORITIES OF THE INDIAN CHURCHES IN THE CONTEXT OF THE GREAT COMMISSION

Kaholi Zhimomi[1]

### 1. Introduction

The world is in flames, Syria the worst affect of all at present. Nations at large are witnessing the highest movement of people in millions after the Word War II. Media flashes the plight of displaced people across the globe seeking out for refuge in strange lands. An entire future generation of an ethnic group and the rich heritage of a nation is collapsing under the very gaze of the 21st century generation. In retrospecting our own India, secularism is highly at risk. Religious fundamentalism is gaining momentum in many states. Tensions spread across the country with the "beef ban" controversy and people being lynched for the same. Proliferation of atrocities on women, children, dalits, tribals and adivasis cannot be ignored. While the public turn to the Capital for answers the present ruling government play the "development" card dismissing the issue all together. The very system that is meant to protect does actually the opposite of it causing intense fear to its citizens at the margins leaving many to wonder of the unclear impending future. Conflicts in ideas and divisions based on religion, caste and

1 Dr. Kaholi Zhimomi is a Lecturer in the Department of History of Christianity at the United Theological College, Bangalore.

politics have manoeuvred the country towards dissension. Where then can the Indian churches be mapped within this gigantic Hindu setting? Apparently India being multidimensional in one hue or the other, the Indian churches can be located in the midst of this milieu having to always struggle to survive as minor groups. Indian churches under the Bharatiya Janata Party (BJP) led government have come under the microscopic lens being dissected at every turn. Looking at the present world scenario particularly religious India, Christians are confronted with the task of continuing God's Mission (*Missio Dei*) in witnessing to Christ. In this context how can the churches' Ecumenical priorities be revisited to fulfil the "Great Commission"?

## 2. 19th Century Slogan, "The Evangelization of the World in this Generation"

The urgent need for unity and co-operation in the mission fields resulted in various consultative mission conferences not only in Europe and America but also in Asia and Africa throughout 19th century. The missionaries' search for unity and spread of the gospel made denominational division less important and they strived to be bonded together by one common faith. International gatherings were organized for the churches to come together and inspire them for mission and Christian Unity.[2] These Protestant mission works in the 19th century can be characterized as "ecumenical." The ecumenical openness and growing interdenominational cooperation of the 19th century missionary movement made mission the most important catalyst for the 20th century ecumenical movement. The need for "ecumenizing" in mission first became evident in the mission fields. The strongest stimulus to ecumenical missionary cooperation came from the ecumenical youth and student movements, with their famous slogan, "The Evangelization of the World in this Generation," which produced many pioneers of the 20th century ecumenical movement, like John R. Mott, J. H. Oldham and W.A. Visser-t Hooft.[3]

World Missionary Conference held at Edinburgh in 1910 which is known as the cradle of the Protestant world mission and ecumenism in the 20th century became a historical landmark because this marked the transition of the missionary movement from the 19th to 20th century.[4] This conference became significant

2 Kenneth Scott Latourette, "Ecumenical Bearings of the Missionary Movement and the International Missionary Council," *A History of the Ecumenical Movement: 1517- 1948*, edited by Ruth Rouse and Stephen Charles Neill, Vol. 1, 3rd edition (Geneva: World Council of Churches, 1986), pp. 354f.

3 A. Wind, "The Protestant Missionary Movement from 1789 to 1963," *Missiology an Ecumenical Introduction*, edited by F. J. Verstraelen, A. Camps, L. A. Hoedemaker, M. R. Spindler (Grand Rapids, MI: William B. Eerdmans Publishing Company, 1995), pp. 237-242.

4 T. V. Philip, *Edinburgh to Salvador, Twentieth Century Ecumenical Missiology: A Historical Study of the Ecumenical Discussions on Mission* (Thiruvalla, New Delhi: CSS & ISPCK, 1999), p. 23.

because of its influence on mission and the far reaching result of the conference. World Missionary Conference is therefore known as the beginning of the Modern Ecumenical Movement.[5] It also came to be known as "a turning point in human history" and a "spiritual evolution of humankind." Hence, the period after Edinburgh was known as "the most glorious in human history" where "a greater unity of Common action" was attained. This conference was an outcome of determination, perfect obedience to God and surrendering to His will.[6]

## 3. 20th Century Slogan, "Carrying the Gospel to all the Non-Christian World"

One remarkable thing about World Missionary Conference, Edinburgh 1910 is that when the Western world in their struggle for political and economic expansion steered towards division and conflicts, the churches were beginning to grow towards unity and fellowship. Edinburgh 1910 not only brought about world mission and ecumenical movement but brought about the expression of variety of new missiological views.[7] The world was living in denominational barriers and noticed a collapse in the Evangelical Unity which led to the missionaries' attempts to unify the churches in the mission fields. But, it was only in Edinburgh conference did they see promise of unity among the Christians,[8] focusing primarily on church union in places like Asia and Africa. This Conference aimed at mission fields with their core vision, "the whole world is the mission field, and there is no church that is not a church in the Mission field." This vision was later on fulfilled through different councils and conferences.[9]

It became significant because of its influence on mission and the far reaching result but the conference in certain ways motivated the spread of western imperialism and their superior ideology through missionary societies. Of all the reports of the conference the foremost commission was, "Carrying the gospel to all the non-Christian world." The missionary enterprises were zealous in promoting the western scientific rationality brought about by the European Enlightenment. Moreover, the conference could not but subjugate to the colonial project and mission agenda brought about by the colonial administrations.[10]

---

5 T. V. Philip, *Ecumenism in Asia* (Delhi: ISPCK and CSS, 1994), p. 27.

6 Hans Heinrich Wolf, "The Ecumenical Movement," *Twentieth Century Christianity: A Survey of Modern Religious Trends by Leading Churchmen*, edited by Stephen Neill (London: William Collins and Sons Ltd., 1961), p. 382.

7 A. Wind, "The Protestant Missionary Movement from 1789 to 1963," pp. 243f.

8 Stephen C. Neill, *Brothers of Faith: The Story of Men Who have Worked for Christian Unity* (Nashville: Abingdon Press, 1960), p. 16.

9 F. Hrangkhuma, *An Introduction to Church History* (Bangalore: Theological Book Trust, 2002), p. 370.

10 M. P. Joseph, "Revisiting the Edinburgh Conference in the Context of Globalization," *Witnessing in Context: Essays in Honor of Eardley Mendis*, edited by Monica J. Melanchthon

The Christians were to focus not on non-Christian religions but on studying 'the problems involved in the presentation of Christianity to the minds of the non-Christian peoples.'[11] The missionaries were therefore instructed to examine and uncover "point of contact" in non-Christian religions, which can be used to attract the believers of other faiths toward Christianity.[12] With the theme, "Carrying the Gospel to all the Non- Christian World," the world was now divided into the civilized Christian West and the "non- Christian" rest. So, the goal of mission was the Christianization of the entire non- Christian world, with Western culture and the Western church as the model. The conference aimed to plant one undivided church of Christ in the so called non-Christian lands. Missionary societies were considered legitimate means for mission, especially for churches that were not engaged in mission. They emphasized on planning, mission strategy and efficient communication of the gospel. Much of the Edinburgh's optimism came from the fact that it was an age of the western imperialism. The Edinburgh Conference echoed the 19th century missionary interpretation of colonialism.[13]

## 4. 21st Century Slogan, "Witnessing to Christ Today"

After hundred years Christians witnessed the commemoration of the crucial milestone in the history of Protestant missions and the modern ecumenical movement at the centenary celebration. Edinburgh 2010 with the theme, "Witnessing to Christ Today" continued the goal of Christian mission- the *oikumene* of God: "The earth is the Lord's and everything in it, the world and all who live in it" (Psalm 24:1). But, Witnessing to Christ has become the most crucial question facing the Christians today in the 21st century.

India is a multi-faith, multi- culture and multi ideological nation. Witnessing to Christ in these situations come with many barriers. India is a country with a majority of Hindus dominating the Muslims and the Christians. These groups politicize religion resulting in stripping of secularism in India today. India has felt the impact of communalism and religious fundamentalism since ages but the Babri Masjid[14] incident in 1992 pushed communalism and religious fundamentalism to

---

and George Zachariah (Thiruvalla: Christava Sahitya Samithi, 2007), pp. 156f.

11 World Missionary Conference, Edinburgh 1910, *Report of Commission IV: The Missionary Message in Relation to Non-Christian Religions* (Edinburgh and London: Oliphant, Anderson, & Ferrier, 1910), 1.

12 Brian Stanley, *The World Missionary Conference, Edinburgh 1910* (Grand Rapids, MI and Cambridge: Grand Rapids, MI: William B. Eerdmans Publishing Company, 2009), p. 212.

13 T. V. Philip, *Edinburgh to Salvador, Twentieth Century Ecumenical Missiology: A Historical Study of the Ecumenical Discussions on Mission* (New Delhi: CSS & ISPCK, 1999), pp. 171-174.

14 Hindus destroyed an Islamic mosque on December 6, 1992 in the town of Ayodhya in northern India. Many Hindus believe that Babri Mosque, constructed in the 16th century by the conquering Muslims, was situated on the spot where a Hindu deity, the God Ram, was born 5,000 years ago.

the extent of almost breaking India. The destruction of the mosque at Ayodhya was the most spectacular action by Hindu fundamentalists in the last decade. Their political success has heightened fears that fanatic religious elements are taking over the government. In destroying the mosque the fundamentalists defied the country's constitution. During the last two or three decades, Hindutva and the cultural nationalism in India have affected the inter-religious relations. Communal feelings between Hindu-Muslim and Hindu-Christian hampered the peaceful atmosphere and integration of India.[15]

Recently the Dadri mob lynching case in which the family of Md Akhlaq was attacked by a mob on the night of 28th September over the rumors of beef eating at a Dadri village in Greater Noida, Uttar Pradesh, shook the nation's very foundations of the Indian constitution. 52 years old Muslim farmer Mohammad Akhlaq was lynched to death and his 22 years old son Danish was beaten up for allegedly eating beef on Eid.[16] This incident has created an atmosphere of suspicion and distrust in the communities. The beef politics following the Dadri lynching disseminated the communal vibe in country.[17] The intelligentsia and large sections of the public have been condemning the food politics which has in several ways threatened the secular ethos of the country. The atmosphere of fanaticism is swelling up in the country with the minorities being harassed both at the individual and institutional level. Several Christian institutions and organizations are now targeted but unfortunately it seems the government has no action plan to check such incidences.

In this situation how can the instruction of the Great Commission be fulfilled and how can the churches involve in Witnessing to Christ? Jesudas M. Athyal observes that Indigenous Indian missionaries during the period of Babri Masjid issue were on the drive towards 'the evangelisation of India,' instead of being in tune with the socio-cultural realities of the 'mission fields.'[18] The aggressive evangelistic campaigns have triggered the Hindu negative approach towards Christianity thus leading to controversies and debates with Hindu religious leaders. The Hindus were moreover critical at the missionary activities and considered Christianity as a colonialist religion.[19] Today, the Indian churches need a shift in witnessing to Christ through networking and dialogue with people of other faiths. Perhaps

---

15 T. Swami Raju, *Christian Responses to Plurality of Religion* (Bangalore: BTESSC/SATHRI, 2006), p. 120.

16 "The Dadri lynching: how events unfold," *The Hindu* (20 October 2015), m.thehindu.com/specials/in-depth.the-dadri-lynching-how-events-unfolded-/article77194.ece (accessed on 23 Oct, 2015).

17 "Clerics urge govt to curb 'hate' peddled by BJP leaders," *Deccan Herald* (Bengaluru), (8 October 2015), p. 8.

18 Jesudas M. Athyal, "Witnessing Christ in a Pluralistic Society," http://jmathyal.tripod.com/id12.html (accessed on 7 October 2010).

19 T. Swami Raju, *Christian Responses to Plurality of Religion*, p. 56.

the greatest challenge facing the churches today is the very religious, political and social structures that bring dissent. The secular structures are contested by the Hindu majoritarian view seeking to impose their ideology on the rest of the minor groups in the country.

## 5. Can "The Great Commission" be fulfilled in this Context?

In the religious context, cultural pluralism has had far-reaching effects. The ideology of cultural pluralism does not meet with ready acceptance when religion is involved. The biblical injunction to disciple all nations tend to engender an assimilationist attitude towards people of other faiths. In the context of the "Great Commission" many Christians have been preconceived to think of their proper role as Christians is to convert and incorporate outsiders into the Christian fold.[20] Athyal in his article, "Witnessing Christ in a Pluralistic Society," observed that in a pluralistic context such as India "the search for relevant patterns of Christian witness in most cases is also an encounter between the Christian faith and other faiths, raising questions of gospel and culture at the theological level." What then is the meaning and scope of witness in a pluralistic context? While relating to the "Great Commission" and "how do we relate the mandate (the text - Bible) to the context?"[21] During the last decade India has witnessed certain specific historically based issues which have sensitized the Christian missions to change their pattern of Christian witnessing and to seek for a relevant model. India has become more complex and critical in the subject of propagating the gospel.[22]

Amidst conflict and challenges between Christianity and Hinduism in the 19th, 20th century there a shift in the mission and model developed called the "inter-faith dialogue." This helped resolve conflicts among multi-religious and multi-cultural communities such as India. It led to mutual sharing and an opportunity for Christians to share their faith-experiences and listen to people of other faiths.[23] Keeping in mind this line of thought many Indian Christians especially converts from Hindu faith are in a process of dialogue with Hindu-faith experiences. These dialogues have resulted in many new reflections in the light of God and Jesus paving way for Christians to witness Christ to the Hindus and other faiths. Indian Christian theologians have interpreted a certain number of Christian values and teachings in the light of other religious faiths.[24]

Serious efforts were made by Christians to dialogue with people of other faiths but controversial issues in the teachings of Christianity by people of other faiths

---

20 John G. Strelan, "The Age of Pluralism," Concordia Journal (July 1990), pp. 208f.

21 Jesudas M. Athyal, "Witnessing Christ in a Pluralistic Society," http://jmathyal.tripod.com/id12.html (accessed on 7 October 2010).

22 Ibid.

23 T. Swami Raju, *Christian Responses to Plurality of Religion*, pp. 44f.

24 K. P. Aleaz, *Dialogical Theologies: Hartford Papers and Other Essays* (Kolkata: Punthi Pustak, 2004), pp. 111-126.

such as- the uniqueness of Christ, Salvation, mission and evangelism, baptism and conversion challenged the core of Christianity. Nevertheless, dialogue model was a legitimate attempt on the part of the Christians in order to build mutual understanding and a healthy relation with the people of other faiths.[25]

## 6. Churches' Ecumenical Priorities to address the Oppressive Structures

M. M. Thomas in his article, "Christian Ecumenism for the renewal of secularism in India," quoted:

> In a pluralistic situation, which is now everywhere in the world, human neighbourhood community can be based only on an open secularism, that is, a secular anthropology open to and reinforced by different religions, ideologies and cultures. And Christ- centred humanism has the best opening of making its impact in this dialogic social existence.[26]

Every religion has its own specific tools of spirituality therefore religious leaders of various faiths and denominations should identify those in their respective religions, such as truth, compassion, justice, equality and address the problem of poverty and socio-economic disparity squarely. There is a need to fight against casteism, communalism, consumerism, gender inequality and child slavery. Swami Agnivesh in his lecture on "Confessing Faith in Action in a Pluralistic Society" observed that "in the realm of religion, we need to go beyond cosmetic dialogue. We need to encourage and promote the freedom to doubt, to debate and to dissent."[27]

India should be looked from the view point of new social movements, the women, dalits, adivasis, tribals, poor, human rights, environment, culture and religion. One of the greatest challenges that face the Christian mission today is the Indian rural poverty. One out of every three persons in India is poor. They have no power to determine their economic development and social mobility. Poverty is not only the lack of empowerment, knowledge, opportunity and basic needs but also a sense of powerlessness and deprivation of entitlement.[28] James Massey noted that in continuing this journey of participating in God's Mission partnership and relationship with neighbours of other faith is necessary. The

---

25 T. Swami Raju, *Christian Responses to Plurality of Religion*, p. 117.

26 M. M. Thomas, "Christian Ecumenism for the renewal of secularism in India," *Ecumenism: Hope in Action: Essays in honour of Dr. Mathai Zachariah*, edited by Aruna Gnanadason (Nagpur: NCCI, 1990), p. 105.

27 Transcending Boundaries for a true Ecumenism, *Report of the Consultation held in Honour of Rev. Dr. Satish C. Gyan on his 60th Birthday (1997)* (Raipur: Raipur Churches Development & Relief Committee, 1998), p. 11.

28 Samuel Jayakumar, "Transforming the Indian Culture of Poverty and Oppression," *Dharma Deepika* 13/2 (July-December, 2009), pp. 45f.

contextual experience and struggles of the people need to be considered along with the academic settings. The unity shared as Christians through Christ in God's Mission must stimulate partnership and network with people of other faiths and civil society in addressing the contemporary challenges alarming the world. The churches should be advocates in questioning the oppressive structures in churches and society.[29]

## 7. Implications, Challenges and Questions

The current settings testify to the shift from distinguishing between Christian world and the world of people of other faiths to recognizing a global world. Although we talk of the global world, Christians and people of other faiths appear to be living in quite separate worlds. Buddhists, Hindus, and Muslims have relatively little contact with Christians. What can the Christians do to restore this correlation? The challenges that further augment here is how can the churches witness to Christ in a context when the common Indians are still struggle for their basic rights? How can Christian churches fight for their rights? How can Christian faith become meaningful to this group of people? These are some of the pertinent queries that need to be addressed while moving together as Christian community in fulfilling the task of the "Great Commission."

At the report of Commission IV at Edinburgh 1910 mission was that of comparing, contrasting, or relating the Christian religion to other religions. But today 'Christian mission among other faiths' cannot be carried out without keeping in mind the various backgrounds and traditions. Christian witness cannot be conceived without acknowledging the plurality of religions and cultures in India. There is a need for referring to the religious and cultural experiences of people of other faiths in order to witness Christ. Every faith has its own strong testament and therefore Christians should acknowledge this and bestow genuine respect on other faiths. Christians in India form only a small minority comparing to a large percentage of Hindus therefore there is always a feeling of communal minority. But, however small the percentage might be Indian churches have certainly made their presence felt in the greater Indian religious and social structure. It has come to the notice of the wider section of the Indian society mainly because of the people based approach in communicating the gospel.

Today the Indian churches irrespective of denominational differences and traditions should go beyond the traditional Indian cultural and religious system and recognized themselves with the dalits, adivasis, tribals, women, and the marginalized. There is a call for revisiting the priorities of the Indian churches for constructing an inclusive community. Cohesiveness among the churches for reimagining transformed structures and systems both in the churches and society is indispensable. Remembering the ethos of the 19th century missionary

29 James Massey, Wati Longchar eds., *Edinburgh 2010: Witnessing to Christ Today in India,* (Bangalore, Kolkata: BTESSC/SATHRI, 2011), p. viii.

zeal where the missionaries' search for unity and spread of the gospel made denominational division less important leading to be bonded together by one common faith, the Indian churches also urgently need to unite and co-operate for carrying out Christian mission. The 20th century church unity and fellowship at the very heart of Western political and economic division and conflicts ought to facilitate in stimulating the Indian churches to unify for a common cause in the midst of the political, social and religious tyranny. The churches' witness to Christ as the foundation of all unity and solidarity with the struggles of people is vital in participating to the objective of the "Great Commission" in 21st century India.

*Chapter 12*

# RE-IMAGING ALTAR AND PULPIT
## WORSHIPPING IN THE LIGHT OF THE 'GREAT COMMISSION'

Viji Varghese Eapen[1]

## 1. Introduction

Sacred space is understood as a space where God is encountered in a special or direct way, by virtue of which the very place becomes holy and set apart from ordinary space.[2] Looking from a biblical point of view, any place is worthy to become a sacred space by virtue of a visitation from God. For example, places like Mt. Moriah, for Abraham, Bethel for Jacob became sacred because of God's encounters, and for Moses, God's appearance to him in a burning bush made that landscape holy. In all these instances, we find an overlapping interconnectedness between the sacred and the secular.

This thought strand is reinforced when God asks Moses to make a 'portable sanctuary' where God would dwell in the midst of His people. God does not prefer to become an 'institution' rather to be a 'movement', accompanying His people through the wilderness as they move toward Canan, the Promised Land. However,

1 Rev. Viji Varghese Eapen is In-charge of the Bicentenary Projects and Programme Promotion of the Madhya Kerala Diocese of the Church of South India.

2 Leland Ryken, James C. Wilhoit and Trember Longman, *Dictionary of Biblical Imagery* (Secunderabad: Authentic Books, 2006), pp. 748-749.

as years pass, there seem to have evolved a different notion that dichotomized sacred from the secular and holy from the unholy, making YHWH and the Jewish religion an institution, more than being a movement. The 'tabernacle' and the 'temple', where God chose to be His 'dwelling place', appear to be the supreme sacred places, where boundaries were strictly observed, protected from improper entry, with the 'holy of the holies' becoming the most sacred space of all.

> "But you shall seek the place that the Lord your God will choose out of all your tribes as His habitation to put His name there. You shall go there, bringing there your burnt offerings and your sacrifices, your tithes and your donations, your votive gifts, your free-will offerings and the firstlings of your herd and flocks." (Deut. $12^{5-6}$) (Also see Deut. $12^{13,14}$).

Later, when the temple was built during the time of Solomon, even the worship seems to have been institutionalized and ritualized, and Solomon seems to have had his own 'temple politics' behind this. Solomon, who had an elder half-brother, was not the real legal heir to the throne, but through shrewd scheming he became king. Soon after he gained control he executed Adonijah and all his potential opponents including Joab (David's top general) and powerful priests like Abiathar were sent into exile. He reorganized social, political and military structures to centralize power, and he also instituted a policy of forced labour for his twenty-year building project of constructing the temple and his palace.

The construction of the Temple played a major role in strengthening Solomon's power, allowing him to control the religious practices as they got centered in one place. It is clear that the Temple too was a way for him to contain God. He said, "I have built You an exalted house, a place for You to dwell in forever." (1 Kings $8^{13}$). Solomon, by building up his empire and the Temple, seems to have subordinated God's sovereignty to His own. And of course, he desired to hold on to power to dominate others, to have a safe and controlled religion, with all its rituals, liturgy and prayers, no more being liberative in its essence and experience.

To get a clearer picture, one needs to look into two important components of this institutionalized Temple, namely the Altar and the Ark.

## 2. Altar

Altar brings to our minds the idea of sacrifice and slaughter, and in fact, the Hebrew word 'Altar' is *mizbeah* which comes from the word for slaughter, *zabah*. However, besides this altar of sacrifice in the courtyard of the temple, there were two other altars inside the sanctuary, one for the offering of incenses and the other for the perpetual offering of the 'bread of the presence.'[3] Though the history of sacrifice and altar could be traced back to the beginning of the human race, to

---

3 Leland Ryken, James C. Wilhoit and Tremper Longman, *Dictionary of Biblical Imagery* (Secunderabad: Authentic Books, 2006), pp. 20-21.

understand the progressive element of the altar in the Old Testament, one needs to go through the descriptions of altars elucidated in the Covenant Code (Ex. 20 - 23), Priestly Code (Ex. 25[1] - 31[11] & Lev. 1 - 16), Holiness Code (Lev. 17 - 27) and Deuteronomic Code (Deut. 12 - 16).[4]

The **Covenant Code** speaks about two types of altars, a *common altar* to which all were to go three times a year to offer the sacrifice and the *private altars* which were permitted on the condition that they may be of unhewed stone or earth. The reason for this condition could be to prevent any permanent sanctuary being established in opposition to the one sanctuary. The **Priestly Code** explicitly mentions that all fat and blood were to be offered there and hence this could implicitly mean, there still existed private altars. The **Holiness Code** and the **Deuteronomic Code** state that every killing of an animal is a sacrifice and hence had to be brought to the one altar situated in the middle of the Israelite camp.

This presupposes that all private altars were abolished. This should have been to centralize everything: one temple, one priesthood, one God, one nation and one law.[5] Before Solomon constructed the Temple as a central element of his efforts to centralize the power, the tribes of Israel had worshipped in a number of sanctuaries and now all these ceased to exist. Therefore, now all Israelites were to come to the main sanctuary to offer burnt sacrifices which became the focus of Israelite worship. The religious institution degenerated through his successors, not to forget kings like Hezkiah and Joash who attempted to reform the religion.

## 3. Ark of the Covenant

One of the sanctuaries in Israel, called Siloh, was destroyed by Philistines, who took from them the Ark of the Covenant. The Israelites eventually regained the Ark, but established it in Jerusalem. David and Solomon desired to have a place where the Ark would be housed as the basis of constructing a Temple. After the construction of the Temple, the Priests and the Levites brought in the 'portable' Ark of the Lord, the tent of meeting, and all the holy vessels and placed them inside the temple. (1 Kings 8[1-13]).

The Ark of the Covenant had four parts namely, the Ark proper, the mercy seat, the cherubim and the shekinah.[6] The **Ark proper** contained the Ten Commandments (Deut. 10[1-5]) and of course, manna of the wilderness (Deut. 31[26]) and Aaron's budding staff.[7] Though the **mercy seat** was just a cover, it was the place where God showed Himself merciful in forgiving the Sin. The **Cherubim**, two gold figures, made of the same piece of gold as the mercy seat kept gazing with the

4 Peter J. Riga, 'Origins and Meaning of the Christian Altar', in *The American Ecclesiastical Review* (The Catholic University Press, August 1963), pp. 100-122.

5 Ibid.

6 William Brown, *The Tabernacle, its Priests and its Services* (Massachussets: Hendrickson Publishers, 1996), pp. 73-83.

7 Leland Ryken, James C. Wilhoit and Trember Longman, ..., pp. 42-43.

most intense and delighted interest on the blood sprinkled mercy seat. (Ex. $25^{20}$). The **Shekinah** was the name given to the visible manifestation of God's presence, filling the space between the mercy seat and the wings of the Cherubim.

The fact that many who looked into it were smitten (1 Sam. $6^{19-21}$), it overthrew Dagon, the god of Philistines (1 Sam. $5^{3-5}$), it parted the waves of Jordan and that before it fell the walls of Jericho were enough reasons for its power to be believed and to be venerated. It was moved to Mt. Zion by David (2 Sam. $6^{12-16}$), and later given a resting-place in the Temple of Solomon ( 2 Chron. $5^{5}$), drawing many to worship there.

During the Babylonian captivity, when the Jews were deprived of the Temple services, to gather together to worship as well as to preserve the bond, the institution of Synagogues became needful, and later, even after their return, the synagogues continued to be part of their worship life, growing simultaneous to the services in the Temple. Synagogue worships included prayers, reading of scripture and usually an interpretation or exposition of the text. Important to be noted here is that there was Ark (Torah Ark) in Synagogue where the Book of Law was kept, which was taken and read. Different from the Temple worship, here in the Synagogue there were no sacrifices but preaching, which became integral to the worship.

However, as ages passed, the Altar and Ark represented the degeneration of a worship that was institutionalized, not in any way standing in continuity with the Kin(g)dom values. Jesus Himself had to fight against this kind of religious institutionalization which overlooked the missiological scope of liturgy and worship, which had become very oppressive in its nature. He openly criticized the High Priest, Priests, Pharisees, Sadducees and Scribes, calling them Hypocrites. His 'Cleansing of the Temple' and open criticism against the custom of declaring 'Corban' clearly state hom much was Jesus disturbed with the then temple rituals and practices.

> For Moses said, 'Honor your father and your mother'; and, 'Whoever speaks evil of father or mother must surely die.' But you say that if anyone tells father or mother, 'Whatever support you might have had from me is Corban' (that is, an offering to God) then you no longer permit doing anything for a father or mother, 13 thus making void the word of God through your tradition that you have handed on. And you do many things like this" (Mark $7^{10-13}$).

Jesus and His disciples/Apostles attempted to reform the religion and its practices. Jesus in fact, began His prophetic public ministry to reform the society and religion from the Synagogue in Nazareth, where he declared His manifesto the Lord had anointed Him to preach good news to the poor, to bind up the brokenhearted, to proclaim freedom for the captives and release from darkness for the prisoners to proclaim the year of the Lord's favor. In the New Testament period, not only that Jesus and His disciples went to the Temple, but the first Christians, being converts from Judaism, appropriated many Jewish practices. This could be because Christ was considered by them as the fulfillment of the Jewish Messianic hopes.

However, as more and more non-Jews got admitted into the Church, gradually the Christians abandoned the early attachment to the Jewish cult with its attachment to the temple and its altar and started to have their own worship places. It is clear when St. Paul, in his letter to the Hebrews says, "We have an altar from which those who serve the tabernacle cannot eat." And ultimately the sacrifice in the Altar during the last day of the week was replaced by the Holy Eucharist on the first day of the week, remembering the great sacrifice of the Paschal Lamp, the Jesus Christ.

On the Sabbath, the Synagogue gathered around the Ark to praise, pray and to hear their teaching and meditating on the law and the prophets. This was the type of worship that came into the early Church with preaching from the pulpit also gaining prominence, along with the Eucharist. In short, the 'Ministry of the Breaking of the Bread', represented by 'Altar' which followed the 'Ministry of the Sharing of the Word', represented by 'Pulpit' became the two integral parts of Christian Worship.

Acts $2^{44-47}$ showed signs of a revival of the religion again becoming a movement, with table fellowship and preaching becoming the central acts of worship.

> All who believed were together and held everything in common, and they began selling their property and possessions and distributing the proceeds to everyone, as anyone had need. Every day they continued to gather together by common consent in the temple courts, breaking bread from house to house, sharing their food with glad and humble hearts, praising God and having the good will of all the people. And the Lord was adding to their number every day those who were being saved.

However, this revived hope lasted only until Christianity was declared as the official religion of Rome and soon, this movement too became institutionalized, which was evident in its worship, hierarchy and rituals.

## 4. 'Come and Become Worshipers' or 'Go and Make Disciples'?

A thorough reading of the Bible proves God has been calling and commissioning His people, not just towards worship rather towards discipleship…not towards religion as an institution, rather movement. There are incidents in the Scripture where individuals and communities being called in the midst of worship towards discipleship. Isa. $6^{1-8}$ depicts that kind of worship that challenges an individual towards discipleship, *prophetic ministry*. It begins with the vision of Seraphs with six wings worshipping the Lord, singing, "Holy, Holy, Holy is the Lord of hosts; the whole earth is full of His glory.", proceeding to the confession of Isaiah, leading to the absolution of His sins and ultimately ending with his commitment, "Here am I; Send me."

In fact, Matthew in his gospel, portrays Jesus' life beginning with Him being visited by the wise men from the East, coming towards Jerusalem, guided by a star. When the star stopped, they entered the house, knelt beside Jesus and paid homage, worshipping Him and offering Him the gifts of gold, frankincense and myrrh. And towards the end of the gospel we find the same Jesus praying in Gethsemane that His Father's will be done through Him, making Him a paradigm of true discipleship. Moreover, after proving the cost of discipleship, He calls the eleven disciples and goes to a mountain in Galilee, where they worship Him. But Jesus calls them who were worshipping Him, towards a discipleship and commissions them to go and make disciples.

In fact, the 'Great Commission' seems to allude to Dan. $7^{9-14}$ and Deut. $31^{14-15}$. Jesus, whose favourite title for Himself throughout the gospel has been 'Son of Man' is given all authority on heaven and earth (Matt. $28^{18}$) just as the Son of Man in Daniel's vision received an identical universal authority.[8] In relation to Moses, both Jesus and Moses end their lives on mountains and God commissions Joshua to succeed Moses, as Jesus commissions His disciples to follow Him. In fact, both these incidents referred in the Books of Daniel and Deuteronomy happen in the context of worship/worship places.

> As I watched in the night visions, I saw one like a human being coming with the clouds of heaven, and he came to the Ancient One and was presented before Him. To Him was given dominion and glory and kingship that all peoples, nations and languages should serve Him (Dan. $7^{13-14}$).

> The Lord said to Moses, "Your time to die is near; call Joshua and present yourself in the tent of meeting, so that I may commission Him." So Joshua and Moses went and presented themselves in the tent of meeting and the Lord appeared at the tent in a pillar of cloud (Deut. $31^{14-15}$).

According to Ireneus, the Church Father, the date of composition of this gospel, which speaks about action, conduct, relationship, justice and love, was composed in 60 CE.[9] 'Great Commission' (Matt. $28^{19-20}$) offers a summary of the whole gospel by weaving together its Christological (Matt. $28^{18}$), ecclesiological (Matt. $28^{19}$) and the eschatological (Matt. $28^{20}$) threads into a carefully crafted

8 G. K. Beale and D. A. Carson, eds., *Commentary on the New Testament Use of the Old Testament* (Grand Rapids: Baker Academic Press, 2007), p. 100.

9 William J. Larkin and Joel F. Williams, eds. *Mission in the New Testament – An Evangelical Approch*, (New York: Orbis Books, 1998), p. 119.

composition.[10] More than proselytization, the call here is to be a community of faith, urging all to follow Christ. What begins here as worship ends as a call towards discipleship. It is a call not to 'come' but 'go', or in other words from the 'centripetal' invitation to a 'centrifugal' commissioning. Therefore, worship has a large scope to mould a community towards genuine discipleship taking across the continuing mission of God. In fact, 'Go and make disciples' is also a reminder to make the Church a movement, and liturgy has its own role in its making.

## 5. 'Missioliturgy': Reading Liturgy in the Light of 'Great Commission'

Throughout its history, though Christianity underwent frequent reform movements, mostly generated by and within monasticism[11], no much importance was given to the reformation of the liturgy, until the 16th Century. The 'Liturgical Reformation' which triggered with Luther's '*The Babylonian Captivity of the Church*' (1520), '*The Misuse of the Mass*' (1521), '*Formula Missae et Communions*' (1523) and '*Deutsche Messe und Gottesdienstes*' (1526) and continued through the works of Martin Bucer, Ulrich Zwingly, John Calvin and Thomas Cranmer, countered many doctrines like 'the doctrine of transubstantiation'[12], 'the idea of sacrifice in the mass'[13] and the 'veneration of the saints.' These reformations to a certain extent also tend to have been a corrective to the false conception of the priesthood, through whom worship during the medieval era had moved from the 'work of the people' (liturgy) to the 'work of the clergy.'[14]

In India too, particularly in Kerala, such liturgical reformation through Palakunnathu Abraham Malpan and Kaithayil Geevarghese Malpan, prompted by their study of the liturgy, Syrian Canon and Bible (not to forget the role of CMS Missionaries) took place in the 19th Century.[15] They urged the church to return to the practices of the 'biblical and unadulterated Syrian Tradition', removing prayers for the dead, prayers to the departed saints and prayer to Virgin Mary.[16] Further,

10 Jacob Kavunkal and F. Krangkhuma, eds., *Bible and Mission in India Today* (Bombay: St. Paul's, 1993), p. 65.

11 Gerhardt B. Ladner, *The Idea of Reform: It's Impact on Christian Thought and Action in the Age of the Fathers* (Cambridge: Harvard University Press, 1960).

12 Robert Joseph Fox, *The Catholic Faith (*Huntington, Ind.: Our Sunday Visitor, 1983), p. 205.

13 T. P. Weber, "Mass", in *Evangelical Dictionary of Theology*, edited by Walter A. Elwell (Grand Rapids: Baker Books) 2001, p. 697.

14 Douglas M. Murray, "Reformed Worship", in *The New West Minister Dictionary of Liturgy and Worship*, edited by Paul Bradshaw (Louisville: Westminster John Knox Press, 2002), pp. 402-403.

15 Sunni E. Mathew, "History of the Development of the Mar Thoma Syrian Liturgy", in *Roots and Wings of Our Liturgy*, edited by A. T. Zachariah (Thiruvalla: Marthoma Annual Clergy Conference, 2008), pp. 19-41.

16 Juhanon Marthoma and Mathews Mar Athanasius, "A Call to the Churches of Christ in India" in ibid.

like Luther had come up with a liturgy in the vernacular (German) language, these reformers translated the liturgy from Syriac to Malayalam. Moreover, the liturgical reformation in India, both in the Catholic Church and the Protestant Church, continued in terms of indigenization and inculturation, the contributory factors being (a) Influence of the National Movements, (b) Indian Christian Theology, (c) Indigenization of Worship, (d) Use of Hindu Religious Terms and (e) Church Union Movements.[17]

On the one hand, all these liturgical reformations seem to have deleted all liturgical elements that they believed were contrary to the biblical teachings and retained only those they found in line with the Scripture. Worship was now founded upon the scriptural authority and biblical principles. In fact, it was after the systematic reading of scripture (*lectio continua*) and its exposition, that the worship proceeded to the consecration and administration of the eucharist.[18] The preaching was made mandatory in order to save the following celebration of the sacrament from being surrounded by superstitions. On the other hand, these reformations made the liturgy more relevant and meaningful to the laity as well as the clergy. The liturgy was made a genuine action of the local church, a living experience of the worshippers and best expression of Church's mystery and mission, including appropriate and meaningful signs.[19] Moreover, the relationship between liturgy and culture was expressed through indigenization, contextualization, adaptation and acculturation of the texts, gestures, postures, objects, time and space. In other words, these reformations were biblical and theological as well as contextual and cultural, pointing out to the commitment of the Church (particularly the Indian Church), to have a liturgy that is authentically Christian and culturally relevant.

At the same time, one cannot overlook the ecclesiological and missiological undertones in these liturgies too. They expounded the *'relatio liturgia ecclesiae'*, relation between the church and liturgy, as liturgy is the church or church is the liturgy. The content of the Church is basically associated with the liturgy. To make it more clear, *"liturgy is the self affirmation of the Church, the manifestation of her very being."*[20] Or in other words, as the classical adage says '*lex orandi, lex credendi*', they articulate concisely, what we worship is what we believe. Liturgy in

17 S. Immanuel David, "The Development of the Concept of Indigenization among Protestant Christians in India from the time of Henry Venn", in *Indian Church History Review* 11/2 (August 1977), pp. 100-102.

18 Douglas M. Murray, "Reformed Worship", in *The New West Minister Dictionary of Liturgy and Worship*, edited by Paul Bradshaw (Louisville: Westminster John Knox Press, 2002), p. 145.

19 The Policy of the CBCI: The National Liturgical Centre as in D.S. Amalorapavadass, in *Toward Indigenization in the Liturgy* (Bangalore: NBCLC, nd.), p. 22.

20 Baby Varghese, "Church as a Worshipping Community: Liturgical Dimensions of Ecclesiology," in *Second International Conference of Ecclessiological Investigations Group* (Orthodox Theological seminary, Kottayam: 2008), p. 4.

fact was believed to convene the Church, through the worship and sacraments.[21] And further, liturgy itself is an action of the Church, where the community of believers celebrates the liturgy. However, the purpose of liturgy is also to make us participate in the mission of God, where, by hearing the Word of God we listen to the history of God's mission as well as receive the call to participate in God's mission. Moreover, towards the end, the worshippers are sent forth to continue God's mission, and hence the liturgies end with a mission mandate.

The current liturgies that we use give ample opportunities to address social causes, one example being the relevance of 'Lectionaries'. Lectionaries, followed by many of the churches in India, includes themes and related scriptural passages for the Sermon, and is strictly based on the salvific act of Jesus Christ, which encourages our Churches to become a moving Church, with missiological emphasis. Liturgically, each cycle is divided into 'incarnational cycle' (Advent to Christmas) and 'paschal cycle' (Lent to Easter) which are linked by the 'Green Sundays' of Epiphany and Pentecost. The themes and passages during each Sundays are related to the respective seasons.

The Advent season is the season of the expectation of Christ Coming into the world. The Word of God, during this season, proclaims the coming of Christ and proclaims that the expectation is fulfilled in Jesus. During the Advent we not only remember the first coming of Jesus but also prepares for His second coming. **While the first coming was as a 'missionary' to us, His second coming is to judge how faithful and fruitful have we been as missionaries, commissioned by Him.**

The season that follows Advent is Christmas. The hope of Salvation of the whole creation is in Jesus the Christ and so we celebrate Christmas. It is the birth of God's only Son into the world. **Through receiving Jesus, we receive redemption, and this is the good news that we proclaim as our mission.**

After Christmas, it is the season of Epiphany, the season of manifestation of Christ. The so called 'gentiles' represented by the wise men, came to Jesus and His glory was manifested to them. **The Church is therefore commissioned to share this glory to many.** During this season, the themes are related to the growth of Jesus and manifesting His glory.

From Epiphany, the Church moves on to the following season of the Lent, and the themes during the Lenten season prepare the believer through prayer, repentance, almsgiving and self-denial for the passion-week, which recalls the events linked to the Passion of Christ and culminates in Easter, the celebration of the Resurrection of Jesus Christ. **This season challenges us, missionaries, to evaluate our missiological commitment, and further calls for a costly discipleship, to take up the cross and follow Him.**

21 George Mathew Kuttiyil, "Salient Features of Liturgy", in *Roots and Wings of Our Liturgy*, Op. cit., p. 42-50.

The following Season begins on the Easter Sunday and extends till Pentecost. During this Season, the Church affirms that Jesus Christ rose again from the dead and through His resurrection; He overcame the old order of sin and consequent death to make all things new in Him. **The church begins proclaiming Jesus as the light of the world, way, truth and life.**

The last Season, which is also the longest Season is Pentecost, starts with Pentecost Sunday or Whitsunday. The Church, basing on the Scripture, believes that the Holy Spirit continued the work of Christ and still continues to transform the creation into the Kingdom of God. During this Season, we meditate upon the growth of Church, Body of Christ, in relation to her specific existential context and time. Therefore, one finds many themes focused towards 'world' such as on witness of Church in the contexts of Globalization and Religious Pluralism, Human Resource Management and Stewardship, Girl Children, Ecology, Youth, Children etc. appearing among the Sunday themes. **The Church is encouraged and challenged to engage in God's mission by responding to all structural evils.**

The eternal presence of Jesus the Christ through the Word and Sacraments, proclaims and promises eternal Salvation and the Kingdom of God without frontiers. The Cycle of Worship and the feast of days end with 'All Saints' Day' and 'All Souls' Day', promising that all the departed will share the very life promised from the foundation of the world. **The cycle of worship, therefore is for the celebration of redemption in Christ and for the fulfillment of the new heaven and the new earth, which infact is our mission, as we participate in the extension of His reign.**

The Eucharist Liturgy should affirm, and reaffirm the missionary impulse in people's hearts and minds, deepen it, and enrich the proclamation that we all must make not only with our voices but with our whole lives. In fact, the church buildings that we have where we worship together should not be seen as a part of infrastructure that brings glory to us, rather our coming together as the Body of Christ in prayer should be seen as a public, evangelical and missionary act. It is a sign to those who see us gathering that we are believers and that this act is so important in terms of our witnessing. Further, we need to look beyond the four walls of the Church to make liturgy our life and our life, a liturgy. In this regard, while we centre our liturgies either or both on Christology and Ecclesiology, it is important to note that the 'Great Commission' calls us to take mission seriously in order to create a liturgy (work of the people) that disciples the church and not a church that disciples the liturgy.

When Martin Luther posted 95 Thesis on the door of the Castle Church in Wittenberg on October 31, 1517, it was not only a dogmatic or theological way of reforming the Church, rather a revolutionary way of equipping the Church to become a community of disciples taking side with the poor. The pope had sent out papal commissioners to sell so-called indulgences, promising forgiveness of sins and access to heaven for everyone, under one condition - cash. The intent was to raise money to rebuild St. Peter's Basilica in Rome, and this forced millions of poor peasants to spend their last pennies, not on feeding their children but instead on buying the "key to heaven" for themselves. Martin Luther protested using pulpits and liturgy (composing chants and songs) against this fraud operation organized by the Church and this became the impetus towards a great reformation including liturgical reformation.

The liturgy of the Word (Pulpit) is a worthy place to be motivated towards mission, since it is the place in which the whole mystery of salvation, culminating in the Gospel, is proclaimed to the assembly of the baptized. This is a time of '**Proclamation**' of the Good News and therefore this time has a missiological significance. What we do with the Word in the liturgy should model our missiological commitment. We are not merely hearers of the Word; we are bearers and proclaimers as well through word and action. Like our proclamation of the Word, our prayers in the liturgy especially, the Eucharistic Prayer has a missiological thrust. Often we understand this prayer as "consecratory," where consecration applies only to the bread and wine. But the fact is it calls the Holy Spirit not only to transform the bread and wine into the Body and Blood of Christ but to transform us as well into the living and effective sign of Christ's Body. We pray that the divine Spirit would transform us like Christ and that use us to fulfill the divine mission because we are the living Body of Christ. Is this not a missiological prayer?

## 6. Conclusion

A relevant liturgy therefore, in the light of 'Great Commission' is a 'missioliturgy' that not only expresses the 'mission of God', but also enhances our missiological commitment, transforming our 'selves' to become in union with Christ, challenging us to participating in God's mission. Such a liturgy would be reforming, refreshing, liberating and empowering, challenging us to transform all structures and systems that legitimize violence, abuse of power, torture, discrimination and inequality. Our worship should continually reform us and bring people together for proclamation and prayer, contemplation, reflection, revolution, confrontation social action, urging people to ask themselves, "Are we a missiological Church?"

## 7. Closing Litany

"We were sleeping when they poured petrol from the window. I smelled the petrol and tried to wake up my wife but by then the fire had started. My children died in the fire," Jitender, father of Vaibhav and Divya, burnt alive in Faridabad.

## 8. Silence

Lord, in a world, tossed and troubled due to war, death, hate and fight, where the body of many are BROKEN…teach us, what does it mean to live Your words,
**"This is my Body, broken for you."**

Lord, in a world, torn, divided and shattered, due to greed, anger and envy, where the blood of many are SHED, teach us, what does it mean to live Your words,
**"This is my Blood, shed for you."**

Remembering Your life, death and resurrection, and remembering the lives of our brothers and sisters in our nation, who are often crucified, tortured, burned and buried, hoping for a resurrection, Lord, we pray, that Your Spirit would be send upon these bread and wine and upon us, Your children, that we would be restored so that we would humbly serve You and spread the gospel of love, all over this nation.

This is the body of Christ, broken for us
**This is also the body of many, broken and crushed.**
**This is also our body, to be broken and be offered.**

This is the blood of Christ, shed for us
**This is also the blood of many, bled and shed.**
**This is also our blood, to be bled and be shed.**

May we become His disciples!
May we go and make disciples!
May be die with Christ, burry with Christ and resurrect with Christ!
May we obey Him and preach the Good News!
May He be with us always, to the very end of the age. **Amen!**

# CONTRIBUTORS

Rev. Dr. P. T. George is a leading Indian missiologist. Presently he is the Principal of the Kerala United Theological Seminary, Trivandrum.

HG Dr. Yuhanon Mor Meletius is the Metropolitan & Bishop of Malankara Orthodox Syrian Church.

Dr. Paulraj Dayanandan is a Professor Emeritus and former Head of the Department of Biology at the Madras Christian College, Chennai.

Prof. Gnana Patrick is the Chairperson of the Department of Christian Studies, University of Madras, Chennai.

Fr. Dr. Jacob Kurian is a Professor Emeritus & Former Principal of the Orthodox Theological Seminary, Kottayam.

Rev. Dr. Sham P. Thomas is a Professor of Communication Studies & Pastor of Primrose Mar Thoma Church, Bangalore.

Mr. Siddhartha is the Founder of the Fireflies Ashram & Intercultural Centre Dinnepalya, Bangalore.

Rev. Dr. Arul Dhas T. is a Senior Chaplain at the Christian Medical College, Vellore.

Rev. Dr. Mervin Shinoj Boas is an Associate Professor in the Department of Theology and Ethics at the United Theological College, Bangalore.

Rev. Dr. K. Jesurathnam is a Professor in the Department of Biblical Studies at the United Theological College, Bangalore.

Dr. Kaholi Zhimomi is a Lecturer in the Department of History of Christianity at the United Theological College, Bangalore.

Rev. Viji Varghese Eapen is In-charge of the Bicentenary Projects and Programme Promotion of the Madhya Kerala Diocese of the Church of South India.